Contents

Jacket: A painting of the Kaiser at
the summit of his power
Front endpaper: Wilhelm as Crown
Prince of Prussia with his wife and
three eldest sons
Rear endpaper: A last tribute from
Adolf Hitler, ruler of the Third
Reich, to the Kaiser of the Second

Copyright © 1970: Harold Kurtz
First published 1970 by
Macdonald Unit 75
St Giles House 49 Poland St London W 1
in the British Commonwealth and
American Heritage Press
551 Fifth Avenue New York NY 10017
in the United States of America
Library of Congress Card Catalogue
Number: 70-83793
Made and printed in Great Britain by
Purnell & Sons Ltd Paulton Somerset

THE SECOND REICH

Kaiser Wilhelm II and his Germany

Harold Kurtz

American Heritage Press

In a Railway Carriage

In 1909, the twenty-first year of Kaiser Wilhelm's reign, a group of German industrialists were travelling along the Rhine. In one corner of the railway compartment sat Walter Rathenau, Jewish patrician and wealthy head of the great electro-technical combine, the AEG, and member of the board of another sixty or so industrial and finance companies in Germany and abroad. Ten years after that railway journey through the Rhineland, Rathenau still remembered the conversation he had had that day with his fellow-organisers of German prosperity:

'They talked about the Kaiser,' he tells us, 'in the manner that was then becoming fashionable – intemperately, bitterly. I said: "Is it chivalrous to hold the man rather than the institution responsible? When did the Kaiser ever overstep the limits of his constitutional rights? By all means draw those limits more narrowly – you and your National Liberal Party have the power and the monarch will always accept an accomplished fact."

'"Why don't you write something about all that?" one of them asked. "After all, you write books."

'"I already write about it twice a year, but permit me to ask you a question. When next it occurs to me to bring the subject up in a petition to Kaiser and Reichstag, will you add your signatures?"

'"Why not? Certainly, certainly," they all exclaimed.

'"You are wrong. None of you will sign, because all prospects of being sent to the Upper House, or given patents of nobility, would be at an end. Your sons' careers would be finished. No further invitation would come from court and its dignitaries would cut you."

'Not one of them contradicted me [Rathenau concludes his reminiscence]. The German upper bourgeoisie knew it to be true, wanted it like that, and confined itself to verbal criticism.'

While his travelling companions were respectable and respected members of the National Liberal Party in which big business and patriotism set the tone, Rathenau was

Left: *Germany's first family. This sort of cosy photograph of the Imperial family sold by the million throughout Germany*

something of a lone wolf, an outsider in the cliquish world of the Second Reich, the others' superior in his wide-ranging and complex interests of intellect and mind as well as in his versatile activities as philosopher, scientist, writer, publicist, and practising artist and musician. Aware of his position as a Jew in Wilhelminian society, it was not until after the war that he took upon himself the responsibilities of political office. He was murdered in 1922 by young German racialists. For all his inner conflicts and contradictions, his was a powerful, almost mesmerising personality, and between 1901 and 1914 the Kaiser received him some twenty times, sometimes in the privacy of the Imperial study, frequently for several hours at a time.

It was a significant little episode, throwing much light on all kinds of aspects of Wilhelminian Germany. In our context, perhaps the most stimulating puzzle is posed by Rathenau's provocative question whether criticism of the Kaiser should be aimed at the flaws and frailties of the man or at the constitutional institutions that made his conduct possible. What sort of a man struggled for breath and self-expression inside the gorgeous uniforms of his high office? To what extent was the personal man identical with, even relevant to the public Imperator Rex who, from the last decade of the 19th century to the high summer of 1914, strode so spectacularly across the horizons of our recent forbears to depart dismally on a damp and dreary November morning in 1918? What temperamental dispositions, what intimate personal experiences, what influences and pressures formed and shaped the man who was destined to combine alarming eminence with shocking failure? The very circumstance of his accession to power, namely the premature and much-debated death of his father, Kaiser Friedrich III, was a European sensation transcending mere dynastic problems. He came into his inheritance before his time: was it the weight and structure of this inheritance, gathered together by Bismarck and squandered by his successors, that forced the Kaiser into the paths of conduct for which he became notorious? Which comes first —the man or the system?

Right: Rathenau, the outsider of the Second Reich (far left), stands watching Chancellor Bülow talking to assorted pillars of Imperial society. Though critical in private of the Kaiser, the German upper middle classes made little attempt to limit Wilhelm II's power, for they knew that all the rewards which they coveted flowed from him and were dependent on his favour

Chapter 1
Born to a Mission

The future Wilhelm II was born in the Hohenzollern Palace in Berlin on 27th January 1859, and from that moment was third in succession to the Prussian throne. King of Prussia was the childless Friedrich Wilhelm IV who in 1859 had already been relegated to the background, a harmless, but hopeless lunatic patently incapable of fulfilling his function as the autocratic ruler of his kingdom and commander-in-chief of its army in the age of democratic restlessness. His brother and heir-apparent, after 1861 Wilhelm I of Prussia, but before this styled Prince of Prussia, had in the year before the baby's birth become Regent. The latter's son, Friedrich, Prussian (and later German) Crown Prince, was the new baby's father. The year before, he had married Victoria, Princess Royal of England and eldest child of Queen Victoria and the Prince Consort. The new-born babe could thus be greeted as a harbinger of Anglo-Prussian friendship, for he was not only Queen Victoria's first grandchild but, to most Prussians, a most welcome guarantee of the continued Hohenzollern presence on the Prussian throne. Baby Wilhelm's mother was, at the time of birth, eighteen, the father twenty-eight, and grandfather Wilhelm sixty-two, while Queen Victoria and Prince Albert were both forty. This eminently satisfactory piece of timing in the orderly procession of generations past, present, and future at the top of Europe's dynastic pyramid was a momentary cause for rejoicing in baby Wilhelm's father- and motherland.

Only the two royal families most closely involved and the doctors and their assistants knew that the birth itself had been so difficult that mother and child barely survived. During two life-long hours, the doctors fought for the mother's life while the baby lay neglected in its cradle and nearly suffocated. Possibly at the last moment, the midwife, Fräulein Stahl, spanked him: 'Breath,' writes Sir John Wheeler-Bennett, 'entered the lungs and the spark of life was saved.'

Left: Friedrich 'the Wise', later Kaiser Friedrich III, with his family. The future Wilhelm II is second from the right

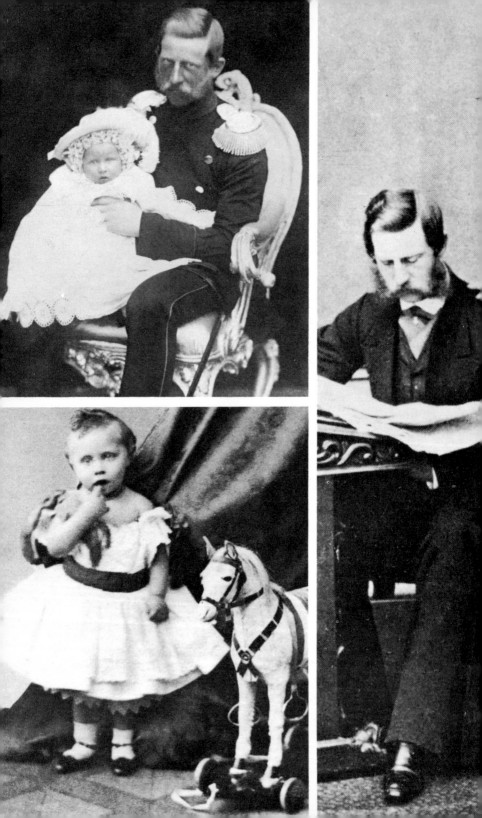

Not before, however, the baby had been badly mauled and deformed during this violent birth. It was found that his head was tilted too far to the left side, producing what modern medical science calls torticollis, a birth injury to the neck. Another neck injury associated with this had damaged the cervical nerve plexus stretching from the neck along the whole length of the left arm. This paralysed that arm and stunted its muscular development from the shoulder to the hand; the limb remained useless and crippled. Finally, the hearing apparatus of the inner ear, the 'labyrinth', was gravely affected, leading not only to deafness of the left ear but, as became obvious some years later, impairing also the balancing mechanism of the semi-circular canals in the brain which lies very close, within a centimetre, to the inner ear. Apart from the crippled arm, the Kaiser's most widely-known handicap, sometimes rather meanly described as his only somatic, or perhaps psychosomatic, problem, the other injuries to his system were only gradually discovered as he grew up and then dealt with by such medical men as won the parents' confidence.

In the state of medical science as it then was, first births were always regarded as especially risky and perilous. To what extent imponderable factors contributed to the exceptional difficulties of Wilhelm's birth — such as the tense and emotionally highly-strung state of his English mother after her first none-too-happy year in Prussian surroundings — is a matter for speculation and guesswork. So is the equally delicate problem of how deeply Wilhelm's temperamental make-up and nervous system was likely to have been affected by the incidence of insanity on both sides of his family. One can only record that three direct ancestors were what we today would call certifiable lunatics. There was, in the first place, his paternal great-great-grandmother, daughter of the notoriously deranged Landgrave Ludwig IX of Hesse-Darmstadt. Then through his mother, Wilhelm was descended from tragic George III, while again through his father he was great-great-grandson of mad Tsar Paul I of Russia, who was released from his raging lunacy by assassination. We cannot say how fatally, if at all, these ancestors reappeared as deleterious influences in the life and conduct of Wilhelm II, any more than we can be quite certain of the permanence or otherwise of the role played by the brain injury at birth.

Left: The 'white hope' of the liberals, Crown Prince Friedrich and his wife Victoria, formerly Princess Royal of England. *Top left:* Crown Prince Friedrich holds baby Willy. *Bottom left:* 'The welcome guarantee of the continued Hohenzollern presence on the Prussian throne', Prince Wilhelm aged two

Overcoming physical deformities and battling on to appear normal was by no means the only task facing little Wilhelm in the years of growing up. Another gift from fate that, as it were, lay in the cradle beside him was his future Anglo-Prussian mission. The marriage between the Prussian Crown Prince and the English Princess Royal to which we owe the existence of Wilhelm II man and boy, had been arranged between the august parents of both victims as long before as 1851. In that year the elder Wilhelm and his wife, Augusta, Tsar Paul of Russia's grand-daughter, were visiting London, ostensibly for the Great Exhibition. They brought with them their eldest son Friedrich, then aged twenty, who on that occasion was permitted to catch a glimpse of a shy and inarticulate young girl aged eleven — Victoria, Princess of Great Britain and Ireland. He returned in 1856, proposed to the now more vocal child and was accepted. Queen Victoria and Prince Albert had worked hard to bring this about, being guided, as they saw it, by the most high-minded and idealistic motives. They were laying their eldest child at the foot of the altar of Anglo-Prussian friendship, and the most curious aspect of the whole ambitious match-making was that both the Queen and Prince Albert worked it through the elder Wilhelm, the Prince of Prussia. They had first come to know him when he was in England in 1848 as a fugitive from the rebellious democrats of Berlin where he had become the best-hated member of the Prussian Royal House and military caste. He was known in Berlin as the 'grape-shot Prince', because he had ordered the Prussian Guards to shoot down the citizens and workers during their demonstrations demanding constitutional reform.

It must be added that the elder Wilhelm was, in everything except army matters, an amiable, courteous, and easy-going man, polished, agreeable to women, unassuming in his style of life, simple in his tastes, unintellectual, and easily amusable. It was only when questions concerning the Prussian sovereign's absolute power over the army arose that he became seized by a strange kind of *ivresse militaire* to remain inaccessible to reason and argument.

Pledge for a liberal future

The Queen and Prince Albert formed a close friendship with a Prince whose solution for economic distress, political serfdom, and inhuman social conditions was bullets, who believed in royal and military absolutism as the sole panacea for all political problems. They welcomed him also as the heir-apparent to Germany's most prestigious throne, and if the Queen and Prince Albert were as opposed to granting concessions

to the mob in the streets as the Prince of Prussia was himself, they were far more sympathetic than he to the German people's thirst for constitutional emancipation and orderly reforms. In their view, Prussia had the mission of uniting under her leadership the other German lands into a *Bund* or Federation and so creating in the heart of Europe a cohesive modern state that would put an end to the debilitating diversity of all those little kingdoms and idyllic principalities which had become Germany since the Congress of Vienna. To give this Prussian mission impetus and force, Prince Albert, and, through him, the Queen, conceived the notion of giving their eldest daughter in marriage to the eventual heir of the Prussian crown as a pledge of their faith in Prussia-Germany's liberal future. The first fruit of this missionary union appeared in this world in the shape of baby Wilhelm.

Queen Victoria and Prince Albert's decision to offer up their daughter to the cause of Germany's liberal future, came from mixed motives, as most human actions do. In the years after 1848 when Louis Philippe of France and his numerous family had arrived in England also as refugees from democracy, and the great Prince Metternich was settling down in Brighton while the revolutionaries of Vienna were being mowed down by Prince Windisch-grätz's guns, the English court found it natural to sympathise with the elder Wilhelm's *ancien régime* side, his Prussian traditionalism, his dynastic outlook—for was Queen Victoria not descended from the Stuarts? The position of Prussia within the concert of Europe was not a strong one in the 1850s, especially in its relationship to Russia and Austria, so that the gain in prestige and *éclat* accumulating from a dynastic link with mighty England promised to be considerable. Thus the new heir to the Prussian crown was, from the second that breath entered his lungs, burdened with a special mission that was intended to give his life and future reign a direction and bias imposed by the older generation.

Left: *Crown Prince Friedrich, now wearing a fearsome beard, taking the waters at Ems with his wife and some close friends*

13

Chapter 2
Inheriting Germany

When the little prince was four, a German doctor offered a brutal contraption designed to force his tilted head into a more natural position. This consisted of a strong girdle worn round the middle of the body to which was fixed a steel rod reaching along the spine up to the neck with a kind of collar in front which gripped the chin and so held the head straight and erect. The stunted arm was treated by all manner of massages and unpleasant electrical treatment, but its muscular development was so poor that little, if anything, could be done about this useless limb. The patient therefore, when a little older, had to accustom himself to using a special set of cutlery at table. His bad hearing was dealt with by hot lotions being poured down the affected left ear at regular intervals.

This tough, prolonged, and often extremely painful treatment of physical deformity produced other difficulties for young Wilhelm. To enter a room, for example, filled with his parents' visitors and guests, cost him for some time a considerable effort, since he was aware of his duty to appear gracious and at ease, shake hands, and keep a flow of small talk going. 'A measured stance, poise in standing, polite phrases, and good manners,' writes Dr Hinzpeter, his private tutor for many years, 'equestrian exercises and conversing in foreign languages – all this he easily learned . . . since intelligent cerebration soon made it clear to him that submission to external discipline was not to be avoided.'

Hinzpeter also wrote as follows of his pupil and 'beloved problem child', in a short pamphlet, that remarkably enough was published in Germany in 1888, the year of Wilhelm's accession:

'Due to an injury at birth which resulted in an incurable weakening of his left arm, a peculiar obstacle was placed across the path of his physical and psychic development. No amount of medical art or care could have removed it, had the child not from an early age co-operated **20** ▷

Left: Bismarck's wars of unification: the Prussian army enters Berlin after victory over Austria and her German allies in 1866

The false dawn of liberalism

In 1848, as in most of Europe, the people of Germany had risen against their rulers. Barricades went up in the streets of Berlin **(right)**, and deaths occurred when troops were sent in to clear them **(far right)**. A democratic German National Assembly, meeting in the Paulskirche in Frankfurt-on-Main **(below)**, offered the crown of a liberal Imperial Germany to Friedrich Wilhelm IV, the King of Prussia. He refused, but felt obliged by popular opinion to grant a constitution to Prussia which abolished censorship and set up a democratic Diet which could scrutinise the actions of most spheres of government except the army. However, this liberal facade was soon eroded by various reactionary decisions. There was a resurgence of hopes for a liberal Prussia when Wilhelm I came to the throne in 1858, but these were finally extinguished in 1862 when the Diet attempted to hold up the military budget and the king called in Bismarck to break its power. **Next page:** The funeral of victims of the 1848 Berlin riots

with quite unusual energy and willpower. The aim was to master feelings of physical clumsiness and the timidity that often goes with them. It was, therefore, a considerable moral achievement for him to become a first-rate shot, swimmer, and horseman . . . The few people who in those early years were able to measure the extent of the whole achievement, of this victory of moral force over physical weakness, have felt ever since that a man like this justified the proudest hopes for the future . . .'

Hinzpeter was in charge of Prince Wilhelm's studies from 1866 to 1877. His regime was an extremely rigorous and Spartan one. Lessons would last twelve hours a day for six days a week. Emphasis was laid on Latin and, later, Greek, 'world history', and mathematics; Hinzpeter implied that his pupil showed himself to be something of an eclectic student, picking out and memorising the things he liked, hardly bothering over uncongenial subjects such as mathematics. The academic programme was rounded off with visits, inevitably, to Berlin's museums and, more sensibly, to mines, workshops, and factories. Possibly most important of all, Hinzpeter taught the Prince how to sit a horse and, more so than anybody else, helped him to correct and overcome both his injured sense of balance (at first the Prince had no sooner mounted than he fell off again on the other side), and learn how to make the best of his crippled left arm.

'What impressed one most in this very good-looking, very girlish boy whose soft delicacy was increased to the point of total frailty by the embarrassing helplessness of the left arm, was the resistance he offered to all pressures, to all attempts to force his inner self into one direction or another . . .' Hinzpeter wrote in his pamphlet. He was impressed by Wilhelm's facility in adjusting himself to the 'tyranny of etiquette which rules the existence of princely families'. He also stresses his pupil's inborn and eager sense of duty, his utter indifference towards the pleasures of this world, and his impeccable submission 'to the authority of school and regiment'. He underlines, possibly a little critically, the Prince's enthusiasm, easily roused by the things that attracted him. He tells us that the preference of the parents tended towards middle-class values rather than military ones, but that the Prince's native military tendencies soon took up a large part of his 'dreaming, thinking, and acting'. Yet, in Hinzpeter's eyes – and there is hardly a more observant or objective witness available for the years between 1866 and Wilhelm's succession as ruler – the army could not claim his undivided attention. Inter-

Right: *The final blow for German unity, King Wilhelm I of Prussia sets out for the Franco-Prussian war on 27th July 1870*

estingly enough, the reason for this Hinzpeter found in
the hostility that army officers felt and showed towards
the navy, which even before 1888 was becoming a chal-
lenging rival claiming equal status.

In a few valedictory sentences concluding the pamphlet,
Hinzpeter says that a sense of duty, 'always the strongest
and most effective motive-power in all members of his
royal race', also dominated Prince Wilhelm's thinking
and endeavours. Moderation, the fight against what
Hinzpeter called 'the passions', self-discipline, self-con-
trol, an inner self-assurance equally remote from 'self-
adulation' as from feelings of inadequacy in the face of
the gigantic tasks of his high office were other qualities
which the tutor professed to discover in the character of
his pupil in the year of his accession. It might be asked
whether Hinzpeter was describing what there was or
what he thought there ought to be.

The tutor's pamphlet, part portrait and part exhorta-
tion, makes it clear that the lively, if somewhat effemin-
ate, Prince was as richly endowed with excellent gifts of
mind and intellect, as he was hindered and inhibited by
the severe physical handicaps with which he had been
born. His quick comprehension, easy absorption, and re-
tentive memory were throughout childhood and adolescence offset by his intense struggle against the almost
degrading weaknesses of his somatic constitution. As a
pupil, Prince Wilhelm showed infinitely greater powers
of application in straining to acquire the physical appearance of the normal, in cultivating a certain prowess
in swimming, playing tennis, sitting a horse, shooting,
than in developing his mental gifts in study.

Prussia rampant
The eighteen years of Prince Wilhelm's childhood and
adolescence had seen his country transformed out of all
recognition. Little Prussia, admired at the time of
Prince Wilhelm's birth for her industrial efficiency, civic
probity, and commercial liberalism, but held in small
regard in the field of power politics and international
relations, had in little over a decade become the strongest
military and political power on the European Continent.
By her swift victory over Austria and the lesser German
states in 1866, Prussia had excluded Austria from her
hitherto dominant position within the German states. By
the equally swift defeat of Napoleonic France in 1870
she had, in one blow, destroyed Napoleon III's position as
arbiter of European affairs and united the kingdoms and
principalities of the two Germanies into a new Reich with
the King of Prussia as German Kaiser. On the tip of the
European scales now sat the Prussian eagle. Little Prince
Wilhelm, then aged eleven, was allowed to head the

victory parade of June 1871 immediately behind his
father and grandfather, when the victorious German
army entered the heart of Berlin through the Brandenburg Gate. In his life-time Berlin was to witness no such
day of roaring enthusiasm again until 4th August 1914.

The Reich that Prince Wilhelm was one day to inherit
had been proclaimed in distant Versailles, far beyond
his vision. Nor could a boy of eleven be expected to
grasp more than dimly the significance of the fact that
his grandfather had left Berlin a king and returned an
Emperor. He received his first vivid impressions of the
increase in parade, ostentation, and outward splendour
that marked the early years of the infant Empire, but
otherwise he still had a good way to go until he could
make closer acquaintance with the dynamically transformed fatherland that he was to rule at some future
date. His tortured and, on the whole, unhappy childhood continued. Only very gradually were the atrocious
experiments discontinued, by which the parents, and
especially his English mother, endeavoured artificially
to put right the injuries he had sustained at birth.

Deeply unnerving and disturbing as these experiences
were for a boy already undergoing the trials of growing
up, they were not by any means the heaviest cross he
had to carry. If we want to see Prince Wilhelm as he was
being groomed and prepared for the first position in an
empire that had so suddenly shot up into the mightiest
position on the Continent, we must fully grasp the fact
that he grew up against a disruptive family background
— a boy whom both his parents had rejected.

His father, Crown Prince Friedrich, was a man of sensi-
bility, intelligence, liberal tendencies, and weak character. Leaving aside for a moment his dynastic position
as a Hohenzollern prince in direct line of succession, we
may see in him a typical product of the generation that
was born after the end of the Napoleonic wars and had
reached maturity before the beginning of the Bismarck
wars of the 1860s. Friedrich, who had been born in 1831,
grew to manhood in the years following the risings and
demonstrations of 1848-49. These movements fell short,
by a long way, of their principal target of establishing the
supremacy of constitutional and parliamentary government over the prerogatives of the crown and its army.
Even so, however, in 1850 a reluctant king had granted
his subjects a constitution of sorts, and Berlin society, to
which even parliamentarians of a liberal tinge were now
being increasingly admitted, saw in this a first move in
the right direction — the beginning of a 'New Era'.

Left: *Prussian troops leave for the campaign against France*

23

Crown Prince Friedrich's generation grew up in a country from which the constitution had at long last lifted the degrading tutelage of censorship of the spoken and written word. The government, for the first time in Prussian history, had a proper opposition that grew in number and influence with every new election. Police and bureaucracy were engaged on a defensive rearguard action, while the army, the third pillar supporting the crown, saw itself compelled to maintain its influence at the top not by open assertion and unchallenged supremacy as hitherto, but by forming a *camarilla* at court which sealed off the king hermetically from all danger of infection by the virus of democracy. From their vantage point off-stage, they observed in alarm, but by no means in passive resignation, the inexorable spread of liberalism in society and public life, a phenomenon which the military and bureaucratic aristocracy of the older generation continued to equate with godless, and ultimately kingless, anarchy and revolution.

The issue of military autocracy versus liberalism finally came to a head in 1862, the last year of the New Era and the third year of little Prince Wilhelm's life. In the elections of March, the radicals who had seceded from the tamer groups of the old Liberal Party to form the German Progressive Party (DFP), had received a record number of votes; in the Prussian Diet liberal representation now stood at 333, as against 15 conservatives. The Chamber flatly turned down all military appropriations of the budget, the conservative minority government resigned; Wilhelm I, more convinced than ever that the parliamentarians were bent on 'ruining the army in its state of readiness, its military spirit, its training', was torn between abdication and sending for Count Otto von Bismarck, a strong-willed Prussian aristocrat and currently Minister in Paris, whom he disliked but who would know how to deal with recalcitrant parliamentary majorities. In this situation he invited his son and heir to call on him.

Crown Prince Friedrich had, especially since his marriage, become identified with the new climate of constitutionalism and liberalism. The historic confrontation between father and son, sixty-five the first, thirty-one the other, took place on 18th September 1862. The embarrassed military autocrat showed the champion of liberalism the instrument of abdication: 'Here is the document, it only needs my signature.' The Crown Prince was horrified. After an emotional appeal from **29** ▷

Top right: Prussians in action against the Danes in April 1864.
Bottom right: Prussia's opponents, French dragoons in camp.
Next page: 1870; Bismarck escorts Napoleon III into captivity

24

father to son, he remembered his own dynastic position and exclaimed: 'It would be a very dangerous precedent for the future, if the Sovereign were to abdicate on account of decisions by the Chamber.' Overwhelmed by what he regarded as the biggest threat that had ever faced the House of Hohenzollern, he rushed from pillar to post to enlist support from all whom he reckoned might dissuade his father from taking the fateful step. He next wrote to his wife, then staying with her mother, Queen Victoria, at some Rhenish castle, describing these unmanning events. The replies he received were more than he had bargained for.

Faced, as she rightly saw it, with the alternative of 'either Bismarck or ourselves', Crown Princess Friedrich felt not even the most fleeting doubt that the only possible answer was to encourage the elderly king's abdication. 'If you advise against it,' she wrote from Reinhardsbrunn, 'you must take the blame if great damage, such as you could have prevented, is done . . . If you do not accept, I believe you will regret it one day . . . If you came to the throne and had a liberal government, the army reform would be saved and I believe that is what your father feels . . . The disagreeable duties we both would have to perform do not count, we must think only of the country and of our children who will one day have to make good where we have failed . . . If only I were a man I could perhaps stand by and help you, but . . .'

The two major prophecies in this letter by *Die Engländerin,* as the Crown Princess was unaffectionately known in the country of her involuntary adoption, came true. Crown Prince Friedrich was to regret his feebleness in the face of beckoning opportunity for the rest of his life. And as Wilhelm II, his eldest-born was certainly forced to make good his father's panic-stricken betrayal in letting government with, instead of against, the people slip through his fingers because it might not be good for the dynasty. That the Kaiser of the future did not seriously tackle this formidable work of reparation until 29th September 1918, when the army saved in 1862 had been defeated beyond the hope of a counterstroke, is one of the major themes in our present study of the nature and character of Wilhelm II's reign.

The crisis of autumn 1862 was solved by Prime Minister Bismarck keeping the crowned *bête noire* of 1848 on the throne against the letter and spirit of the fledgling Prussian constitution. There was a public protest from the Crown Prince when in the following year Bismarck unconstitutionally restored the suspended censorship. **32**▷

Left: Wilhelm I is proclaimed German Emperor by Bismarck in Louis XIV's magnificent palace at Versailles on 18th January 1871

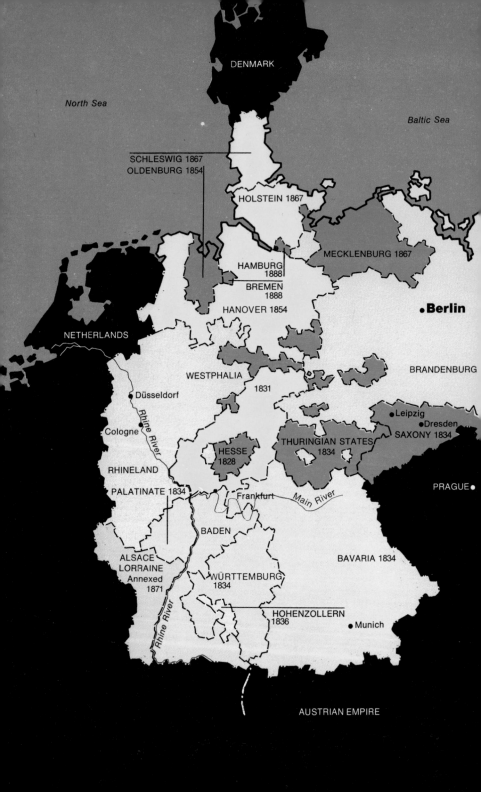

EAST PRUSSIA

WEST PRUSSIA

POMERANIA

SILESIA

Prussia before 1865

Until the beginning of the 19th century, Germany was a patch-work of small independent states. The process of unification was begun by Napoleon after he defeated Prussia in 1806, and it continued after his downfall. The dates on this map show when the various German states joined Prussia, the largest, in a customs union known as the Zollverein. Internal customs barriers which had survived from the 18th century disappeared and the whole area became a free-trading system under Prussian leadership. Politically the area was divided between Prussia and Austria but Prussian economic leadership meant that more and more countries were becoming closely tied to her. In 1865, after the war with Denmark, Schleswig was administered by Prussia.

Prussia after the war of 1866

In 1866 after her victory over Austria and her German allies Prussia annexed Hanover, Schleswig, Holstein, Frankfurt-am-Main, and other minor states.

North German Confederation 1866-70

The remaining states north of the Main were formed into the North German Confederation which excluded Austria and of which the King of Prussia was president. The countries south of the Main were tied to Prussia by treaties

The German Empire

Victory over France in 1870 gave final impetus to unification. The empire was theoretically an alliance of equal states whose leader happened to be the King of Prussia. Each state retained its own ruler and government for internal affairs, and sent an ambassador to Berlin, but in reality they were dominated by Prussia.

The king thought of locking his son up in a fortress but Bismarck, always moderate in victory, thought a stern reprimand should suffice. The Crown Prince had to promise his father never to attack 'my government' again: Friedrich gave and kept his promise. Henceforth, his principal oppositional activity consisted in keeping a secret diary and, like the military *camarilla* in the 1850s, building for his own future in the dark labyrinth below the teeming Prussian ant-heap.

Bismarck soon changed all this. The new public role which with much astuteness he succeeded in creating for the liberal Crown Prince was that of a splendid and heroic leader of armies. In the three wars of the 1860s against Denmark, Austria-Hungary, and France which Bismarck, to quote his own testimony, regarded as a necessity for his policy of uniting the German 'tribes' (again his own expression) into one Reich, the Crown Prince of Prussia was put into the way of victorious military achievement. His public image was clad in the shining breast-plate of the warrior prince, always at the head of his armies, always marching with all dispatch to the scene of battle and so winning new laurels for the glory of Prussia and the House of Hohenzollern.

When in 1864 the Danes had been thrown out of the fortifications of Düppel, the victorious Crown Prince noted in his diary: 'It is true we have a wonderful army, but where will victories under Bismarck lead us? That is the crushing question.' Publicly, however, he was invested with the Order of the Red Eagle. On the evening after Königgrätz, which knocked Austria out of the war and the Germanic system, Friedrich wrote: 'War is a frightful thing, and the civilian who brings it about with a stroke of the pen has no idea of what he is preparing.' On the battlefield next morning, Wilhelm I presented his son with the Order of *Pour le Mérite,* Prussia's highest award. 'We can only mourn,' wrote the unhappy man secretly that day.

By the time the armies of the North German League and their south German allies set out against France in July 1870, the gleaming figure of the Crown Prince on horseback was indelibly fixed in most all-German eyes. It symbolised another transformation achieved by Bismarck in these same years. It had dawned on the Berlin parliamentarians who had hitherto opposed Wilhelm I's and Bismarck's army bills and budgets that the army, having formerly been regarded as the principal instrument of domestic suppression, had meanwhile been shaped into an efficient and effectual weapon of external conquest and foreign policy. Prussia was becoming strong and internationally respected for the first time since the death of Frederick the Great.

Three months after Königgrätz, leading men of the Progressive Party broke away from that hostile caucus to form the National Liberal Party (whose 1909 representatives we have already met in the prologue). They announced that in domestic affairs they would observe 'the duties of a loyal and vigilant opposition'. They certainly were to prove loyal to the Reich, vigilant in all spheres touching on their immediate interests and as oppositional as a herd of sheep with sleeping sickness.

Spectacular leadership: secret subversion

In the Franco-Prussian War of 1870, the Crown Prince resumed his familiar role of spectacular leadership coupled with secret subversion by diary and correspondence with his English wife. Before returning home for the victory celebrations and the inauguration of the new empire, he became instrumental in adding a foundation stone, or perhaps kingpost, to the edifice planned by Bismarck that was to be of decisive importance to the reign of his son and the future of Germany and Europe.

In the middle of August 1870 the Crown Prince said to an intimate friend, Gustav Freytag: 'My father and I went to Paris for the Great Exhibition of 1867. When the visit of the Emperor of Russia was announced, Napoleon III sent someone along to enquire which order of precedence he, my father, wished to see observed, as Napoleon intended to arrange everything according to the preference of the King of Prussia. My father replied: "The Emperor must take precedence." That,' concluded the Crown Prince, 'no Hohenzollern is ever to say again; it must never be true again of a Hohenzollern.'

'The Crown Prince,' wrote Freytag, 'was a mild and warm-hearted man, humane, and altruistic. But ineradically implanted in his innermost being was the traditional concept of his rank and caste. When on occasion he felt moved to remind others of his status, his bearing became far haughtier than that of any of his fellow princes . . . From this princely pride there grew within him the notion of a new German Kaiserdom, and I feel sure that he was the prime mover and author of the Imperial restoration . . . The Crown Prince persevered with the view that the new Imperial dignity would be properly hallowed only if it appeared as the continuance of the old "Roman" *majestas* . . .'

Crown Prince Friedrich was able to put his majestic notion to his enemy Bismarck on 20th August at Nancy and received the Chancellor's promise of giving it 'benevolent consideration'. At this stage in the war, Bismarck was keeping an open mind on the question of what out-

Left: Prussians crown themselves with the laurels of Paris

33

ward shape Prussian supremacy was to be given within the German Confederation he intended to found. Friedrich's idea of resuscitating the title of German Kaiser at once struck Bismarck as a useful device for rallying the German tribes under a popular and folkish banner. If the 'regenerated Germany' of which Bismarck always spoke after 1866, was to have as its head a Kaiser in succession to the medieval Emperors from Charlemagne to the Hohenstaufens, then its style and title would have to be, not Confederation or *Bund,* but Empire or *Second Reich.* If, finally, Kaiserdom responded to Friedrich's exalted dynastic aspirations, it also answered well to Bismarck's political scheming which aimed at the supremacy of the King of Prussia at the centre and regional autonomy of the other rulers at the periphery. No wonder Bismarck had promised the Crown Prince 'benevolent consideration' and that a temporary *ad hoc* alliance was formed by the statesman and the dynast in this, if in no other, respect.

The institution of the German Kaiser which Prince Wilhelm, then aged eleven plus, was one day to take over had been concocted by the unnatural alliance between the romantic Friedrich and the ruthless realist Bismarck.

Overshadowed by all these gigantic events of Germany's European debut, Prince Wilhelm's boyhood and adolescence had meanwhile taken their unhappy course. 'He is incapable,' his mother had written to Queen Victoria in May, 1870, 'of running fast because he has no sense of balance, he cannot ride, climb, or use a knife at meals . . . I am surprised that despite all this he has such an agreeable temper . . . It is all a severe trial for him and us . . .' There is reason to think that the Crown Princess was feeling her share of the trials more heavily than she did those of her son. Disappointed as she was by her husband's lack of political fibre, reduced to impotent rage and fury at their exclusion from serious governmental business by Bismarck, and deeply pessimistic as her contemplation of the future became while Bismarck established the hegemony of the Junker Party over her own Anglo-Coburg set (in Bismarck's frequent phrase), the physical deformity and afflictions of her eldest son ceased to be a cause for compassion and support, and became one for revulsion and resentment. On occasion, she would call him 'cripple' to his face, sometimes in front of visitors, and the older Wilhelm became, the stronger grew her exasperation with his pathetic infirmities of body. She also realised that the boy showed scarcely any curiosity for the things of the mind she cherished

Right: *The inauguration of the Victory Column in Berlin.* **Far right:** *French and Austrian comments on the new Germany —strutting Prussian (top); overwhelmed Emperor (bottom)*

most, that literature and the liberal arts held no strong appeal for him. She dominated family life at Potsdam's *Neues Palais,* the Crown Prince's official residence, but dominated nothing else in either Prussia or Imperial Germany. At the side of a husband who was a political cypher, the rule of Queen Victoria's daughter over the family home became so strong that young Prince Wilhelm, when choosing a bride for himself in 1881, selected the seemingly humble and provincial Augusta Victoria of the Augustenburg branch of the Schleswig-Holstein family because that demure Princess at any rate seemed to have no gift for domestic domination such as his mother had exercised for so long. Or so he thought.

'He will never become mature'

As a father the Crown Prince took his cue from his wife. When Prince Wilhelm came of age, Friedrich remarked after the ceremony to the Rector of Berlin University, who was also a psychiatrist: 'Don't congratulate me – that boy will never become mature, never come of age. And you call yourself a psychiatrist!'

The situation was aggravated by the ancient Hohenzollern tradition that it was the King and not the Crown Prince who was responsible for Prince Wilhelm's expenditure. Rejected by his parents, Wilhelm, first instinctively and later quite consciously, drifted more and more towards the ambiance of his grandfather whom he genuinely adored and who in turn spoiled the boy.

With the same degree of affection, Wilhelm worshipped his maternal grandmother, Queen Victoria. Emotionally and inwardly, his growing up was orientated towards these two grandparents, while in compulsive reaction to the unresolved and unresolvable conflicts at home he cut out his parents and their generation from his erratically developing awareness.

Crown Princess Friedrich was not an emancipated woman, despite her acute and virile intelligence, her sympathy for liberal and, as she judged, progressive ideas. In her eldest son she saw, not an individual person with certain talents, weaknesses, and needs of his own, but a codicil, as it were, to her father's, the Prince Consort's, last will and testament. It had to be the child's principal task in life to prepare himself as the future ruler of a liberal and constitutional Prussia/Germany in the image of England's political demi-paradise. Among the major misfortunes that darkened Prince Wilhelm's earliest life was Prince Albert's early death in 1861.

The image that Prince Albert held of Prussia during his lifetime had been based on the illusion that liberal and free-trading principles were prevailing between 1848 and 1862 when Prussia appeared to move towards ever-

growing internal liberties and modern government. This as we saw, had been Prince Albert's prime motive in deciding that Vicky, whom he called his ablest private secretary, had better fall in love with Fritz, the Prussian Crown Prince, whose sympathies were to so large an extent on the side of the angels of liberalism, tolerance, and a pro-British foreign policy. Neither his widow, the Queen, nor his orphaned eldest daughter ever allowed for the fact that the Prince, had he lived, might have changed his mind about 'dear little Germany'. The dead man's outdated legacy had to be obeyed at all costs, and the man who paid the heaviest price for this ultimately very costly enterprise, was the future Wilhelm II.

Thus Anglo-German amity and harmony, the major dream of the Queen and her Consort, became for Prince Wilhelm from the beginning an entirely unnatural mould into which he was being forced by a domineering and vehement mother who loved her dead father more than she did her living son. 'It has been the dream of my life,' she once wrote to Queen Victoria, 'to have a son who in soul and mind would be like beloved Papa, his true grandson and also yours . . . but we must take things and people as they are – we cannot fight against nature, even if nature appears to us cruel, perverse, and contradictory . . .' It takes little effort of the imagination to visualise what Wilhelm's upbringing and adolescence must have been like in a household ruled by a mother who had to force herself to treat her eldest son 'as he was' by fighting down her violent resentment of the undoubted fact that Willy had not turned out to be another Prince Albert.

In that sad, emotional, and self-pitying Prussian interior, set in the baroque frame of Potsdam's *Neues Palais,* Friedrich played an entirely negative part. Once the Crown Prince in his armour of the war hero of 1870 had ridden through Berlin's Brandenburg Gate with his twelve-year-old son immediately behind him, Bismarck saw to it that he and his English wife had much to be negative about. Friedrich was appointed Inspector-General of the South German military commands which meant that once a year he made a tour of inspection of military establishments south of the Main. He became 'the Protector of Museums', the kindly and assiduous patron of the arts and crafts. After an attempt on the old Kaiser's life in 1878, he became, for a few months, Deputy-Kaiser and carried out his duties, at the expense of his convictions, to universal satisfaction, including Bismarck's. Then he retired again into the frustrations of private life at the *Neues Palais.*

Left: Reading lesson: Prince Wilhelm with the Crown Princess

Chapter 3
A Life of his Own

In 1877, Prince Wilhelm entered, at the special wish of Kaiser Wilhelm I, the First Regiment of the Guards as a lieutenant and there learned, as it was called even then, the 'Potsdamer Ton', which he never shed at any point of his colourful and spectacular life. He learned little else and the harder side of professional soldiering remained a closed book to him. It had been said of his father that the Crown Prince became an army commander before he had become a real soldier, and it might be said of Wilhelm II that he became Germany's Supreme War Lord, before he knew the first thing about soldiering. This was in strong contrast to old Wilhelm I who was nothing if not a professional expert in army matters.

What was the 'Potsdamer Ton'? It was, in the first place, a tone of voice, a Brandenburg-Berlin accent which marked its numberless practitioners on all, especially social, occasions, as men accustomed to command – a loud, grating, barking, rattling tone of voice, high-pitched and nasal, that cultivated several characteristics of Berlin argot but showed its upper-class quality by its maltreatment of certain vowels and consonants. Together with this went a deliberate and no less affected cruelty to grammar, a strong tendency to degrade the language, a preference for crude and coarse epithets chosen mainly from the animal kingdom such as *Schweinehund* and *Rindvieh* – in a word, a style of speech that found few, if any, parallels elsewhere in its mixture of common slang and devastation of grammar and language. As the Potsdam tone of voice spread through Germany – to other garrisons, to the police, the lower civil service, the schools, and so on, it could not unfairly be described as the official idiom of what came to be called the *Obrigkeitsstaat,* the State in which citizens were divided (among many other such divisions) into those in authority with power to command and those who took orders and obeyed.

Early photographs of Prince Wilhelm in his pre-mustachio days show a sensitive and wistful face and convey some idea of what Hinzpeter was hinting at when he

Left: Making a soldier out of the 18-year-old Prince Wilhelm

39

called his pupil's looks girlish. At his grammar school he had written poetry and a drama. These symptoms, if such they were, of a tenderer and gentler Wilhelm shrank and withered in the eleven years between his joining the Guards and becoming Kaiser in 1888, even as the shy and pale oval of his face became obscured by the manly aggressiveness of his moustache. It would, however, be misleading to think that by becoming a Potsdamer and subsequently a member first of the Bismarck circle and then of the Waldersee-Eulenburg-Bülow clique he became, unambiguously and irrevocably a 'tool', as his mother more than once wrote, 'a more than willing instrument and henchman'. Wilhelm II was never unambiguous, never wholly and irrevocably committed to any group, party, or policy, but changed direction and allegiance almost as frequently as he did his uniforms. In a reign of thirty years he upheld only one ideal, a purely dynastic one, namely the exalted vision of his own God-given inviolability as German Emperor and Hohenzollern ruler who was responsible to no power but God.

Aside from his learning the Potsdam accent, his year of service with the Guards is of interest only in one further respect. Ever since Prussia's victory over the Danes in 1864 which brought the sea-coasts of Holstein and Schleswig under Prussian domination, un-Atlantic Prussia had become a power with considerable maritime aspirations. After 1871, united Germany, particularly under the aegis of National Liberals and some of Crown Prince Friedrich's personal friends, had promoted naval expansion. In the 1870s the Second Reich was still clinging, though with decreasing firmness, to a policy of free trade. Its navy was not yet an instrument of war in the combat against national tariff frontiers and the fortresses of protection.

The new status of the National Liberal German Fleet was officially recognised when the second son of the German Crown Prince, Wilhelm's brother Prince Henry, became a naval cadet at the time when Prince Wilhelm served at Potsdam. Sitting in the mess with his new comrades, Prince Wilhelm soon found that these temporarily unemployed, if otherwise expectant, conquerors of three foreign countries were apt to speak slightingly of the naval arm of the Crown. Were these maritime fellows, that bunch of engineers, Hanseatic merchants, commercial travellers, and swimming instructors seri-

Left from top to bottom: The schoolboy prince and the men who watched over his early years: Hinzpeter, the tutor; Eulenburg, the artistic friend; and Holstein, the foreign policy expert. Far left: Bonn's most prominent student, Prince Wilhelm at the university where he spent about six months

41

ously dreaming of reaching a status equal to that of the army? Wilhelm pulled them up and finally arranged to give them lectures on the importance an Imperial Navy could have in an Imperial Reich, sometimes for hours on end. The sources of the Kaiser's navalism rose in peaceful grounds to be diverted later, by Tirpitz and others, into more hazardous channels.

A secret engagement

Soon after his service with the guards, Prince Wilhelm became engaged. It was, at first, a secret engagement entered, now that he was of age, without any previous warning to anybody. His chosen bride belonged to the Augustenburg branch of the Schleswig-Holstein family that had been toppled from their throne after 1864 when the two Elbe Duchies had been annexed by Bismarck's Prussia. The Augustenburgs led an unexciting existence in their Silesian exile in reduced circumstances. The Princess herself, later to become Kaiserin Augusta Victoria but always called Dona by her German and English relatives, was at the time of the engagement a pleasant-looking, properly-conducted, and seemingly docile young lady of no experience whatever in the world of courts and politics. Prince Wilhelm was favourably impressed by the fact that she was the grand-daughter of Queen Victoria's half-sister Feodora of Hohenlohe-Langenburg and so was more likely to be welcomed at Windsor than at court in Berlin, where the Holstein family were suspect of liberalism and hostility to the Reich. Traditionalists also said that the Holsteins were hardly equal in rank to the Hohenzollerns – they were not even a reigning family.

With surprising rapidity, Wilhelm and Dona wore down grumpiness and opposition in Berlin. The Crown Princess, who had always been a warm defender of the Holsteins, was delighted with her son's choice and gave both of them her generous support. Queen Victoria, after some initial reserve, was much taken with Dona when Wilhelm brought her to England in March 1880. 'I wish as you do,' wrote the Crown Princess to Queen Victoria on 26th March, 'that Willy, before he gets married saw a bit more of the world, although visits to Belgium, Holland, and London did not change his manner of carrying on at home – he cares nothing for sight-seeing, is absolutely uninterested in works of art, does not admire beautiful scenery, and never glances at a guide-book or anything else that would instruct him on the places he visits. Travelling is of no use, it is alien to his character . . .'

Prince Wilhelm entered the decade of the 1880s on an exuberant note of happiness and a mounting sense of personal liberation and independence. Germany's giant Chancellor made, through Emperor Wilhelm I, various

arrangements to promote the young man's training for his future responsibilities. In 1886 Bismarck attached Prince Wilhelm to the Foreign Ministry – a privilege which the Chancellor had so ostentatiously refused Crown Prince Friedrich. Wilhelm's father thereupon sat down and put in writing all his criticisms of, his objections to, the character of his eldest son and heir which hitherto he had more usually confined to verbal barbs and general carping. 'Immature', 'inexperienced', 'overbearing', 'vain and conceited' were some of the things the jealous and frustrated father permitted himself in this effusion. In a conversation at this time, Friedrich taxed his son with keeping his parents in the dark about his relations with the old Emperor. 'But Mama only gets angry,' replied the son reasonably and, at this time, courteously, 'when I express opinions with which she does not agree.' The Crown Prince and his wife were now convinced that their son was enslaved – held in the claws of tiger Bismarck.

This judgment was only partially right. In 1884 and 1886 Prince Wilhelm paid visits to the Tsar at St Petersburg in connection with Bismarck's endeavours to cure Russia of the strong resentment she harboured against the Iron Chancellor ever since the Congress of Berlin. This service did not enslave him to Bismarck's will. It is more relevant to note that on neither occasion did the Prince turn out to be an able diplomat. He babbled away about the anti-Russian attitude of his parents, he warned the Tsar against 'my English uncles'. He even told Alexander III that 'my father is under my mother's thumb and she, in turn, is guided by the Queen of England . . .' When, keeping more closely to his brief, he spoke to the Tsar of Constantinople and the Dardanelles, Alexander replied coldly, 'If I want to take it, I do not require the permission of Prince Bismarck.' Prince Wilhelm also heard an old Russian general speak disparagingly of the 'bad mistake' Bismarck had made at 'this wretched Congress of Berlin . . . we are now forced to depend on that damned French Republic which hates you and is full of revolutionary ideas which, if you and we go to war, will cost us our dynasties . . .'

Although during his Foreign Ministry novitiate, Prince Wilhelm was initiated into the Bismarck system of foreign policy, more decisive influences were exercised on him from elsewhere. General von Waldersee, for example, an ambitious political general, who as such had drawn Bismarck's hostility upon himself, whispered seductive words of 'personal rule', of 'dispersing parliament with a handful of the Guards' into the young Prince's receptive ear. It had been the same Waldersee who by a successful

Left: An official photograph of Prince Wilhelm and his fiancée

coup in 1883 had drastically reduced the powers of the Minister of War, middleman between parliament, General Staff and the Crown, and in all essentials increased those of the Head of the Kaiser's Military Cabinet, i.e. the Crown's personal military adviser who functioned outside the reach of the parties and politicians. After 1883, three mutually independent authorities stood, under the sovereign, at the head of the armed forces: the Chief of Staff, the Head of the Military Cabinet and, last as well as least, the Minister of War. Waldersee himself became Chief of General Staff in 1889 when the aged Moltke, victor in the wars of the 1860s, laid down his office, but some years earlier he had established informal calling terms with Prince Wilhelm who often visited the General and his American wife at their slightly unconventional soirées. The Prince became to some extent permeated with the Waldersee doctrine that 'the French state of affairs where the Minister commands the army' was un-Prussian and un-German but would be avoided only if a strong monarch, as opposed to a constitutional one, personally led the army and Germany towards their great destiny.

Another influential figure to step into the wide vacuum left by the withdrawal of parental backing in Wilhelm's slow adolescence and retarded young manhood, was Count Philipp Eulenburg. Although people who knew him are still alive and his private and political correspondence is now more easily accessible, Eulenburg more than any other creature of the Wilhelminian age strikes us today as an elusive individual almost beyond our comprehension. It is not only that he combined in his person musical and literary talent with political and diplomatic aptitude. Nor can one feel that he becomes more clearly identifiable when one recalls that, although happily married to a loyal wife, and father of a numerous family, he had marked homosexual tendencies. He was not a poseur, not excessively vain or inordinately ambitious, but quite genuinely the product of a minority style, taste, and sophistication that has vanished beyond recall – a soft tread among the jackboots, a subdued voice among the Potsdam barkers, an aesthete among the practical jokers in the Kaiser's entourage, ephemeral, melancholy, and symptomatic. Wilhelm, entirely unaware of Eulenburg's darker side, singled him out for marked favours, calling him Phili, addressing him with the familiar 'Du' and generally showing a strong preference for the company of this gifted and appealing nobleman.

Right: Bismarck's farewell from his feudal and obedient overlord. The architect of Imperial Germany at the deathbed of its first ruler – Kaiser Wilhelm I who died on 16th March 1888

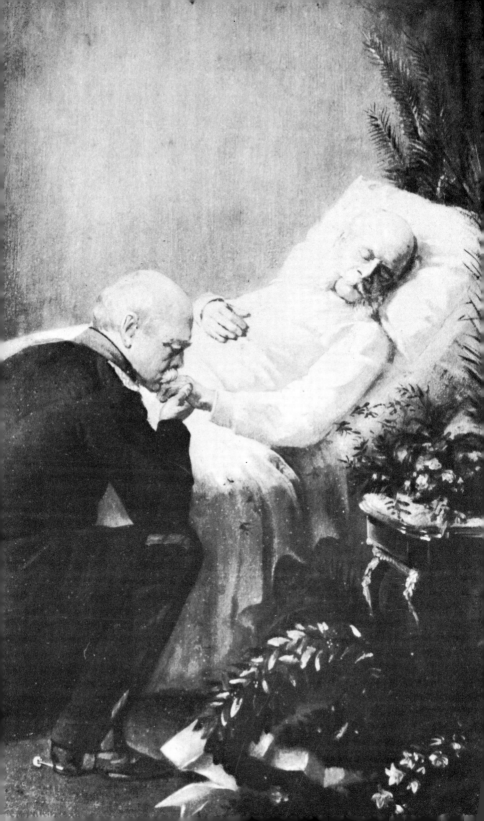

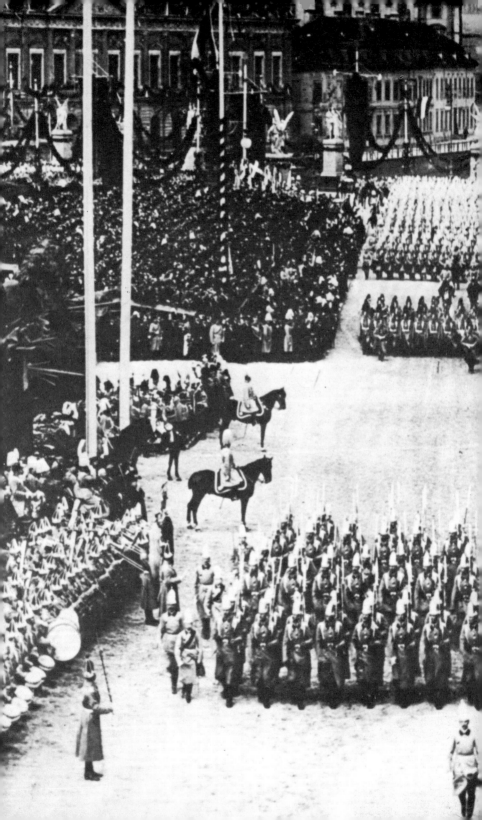

The third member of the group that stood by Prince Wilhelm as he approached ever more closely the steps of the German throne, was the famous Baron von Holstein, virtual, if not nominal, head of the Foreign Ministry in the Wilhelmstrasse. Before his papers were published in the 1950s, more nonsense had been written on this grim and withdrawn civil servant than perhaps on any other figure of the 19th century. He was, of course, a great mystifier and pushed himself so little into the limelight that almost from the moment of his death in 1909 it became absurdly easy to assign to him any role that happened to suit the authors of apologias, memoirs, and other works of self-justification where disinterested objectivity is but rarely the first motive. The fact remains that from the time when Bismarck in 1876 recalled him from his post at the Paris Embassy and installed him in the Wilhelmstrasse, Holstein for the next thirty years remained the confidential adviser of four Chancellors and their foreign ministers. The answer to this riddle without a sphinx is that Holstein was a hard-working Prussian civil servant of the old school with an accumulated knowledge of foreign relations and powers of application which were extremely rare in the Second Reich, never a fertile breeding ground for political and diplomatic talent. Despite his irremovability from his little backroom in the Wilhelmstrasse, he did not direct, but merely advised in, foreign affairs. Although the theory, circulating in his life-time and even now not as defunct as it ought to be — that they did not dare dismiss him, because he knew too many shady secrets and scandals — has in view of the private and public lives of a good many top people in the Second Reich a plausible ring, not one single proof of this low blackmailing side of the *Geheimrat* has come to light since serious historians examined his record from the 1930s onwards.

For reasons which are not entirely clear even today, Holstein and Bismarck broke off personal relations while they were still in office, possibly because Holstein declined the honour of marrying Bismarck's dragonish daughter Marie. At all events when Eulenburg, Waldersee, and others clustered round Prince Wilhelm to groom him in their image for his future reign, Holstein joined the enterprise as counsellor and correspondent.

The old Kaiser celebrated his ninetieth birthday in March 1887; Bismarck, in the same year, had held the highest office under the Crown for just under twenty-five years. Wilhelm I's simple and homely habits, the lack of pomp and exaggeration in his public appearances, the

Left: *The funeral parade of Wilhelm I. His successor, Friedrich III, was too ill from cancer to be able to take the salute*

clocklike regularity of his showing himself daily at the windows of a ground-floor room of the Berlin Schloss at the precise moment when the band of the Guards paraded past in the Unter den Linden outside and Berliners could spot through the window panes a tall, erect, soldierly figure with a blue cornflower on his tunic – all these usefully anodyne details had turned the best hated man in the Berlin of 1848 into a benign and popular *Siegeskaiser,* a loyally acclaimed sight for citizens and subjects.

But viewed from inside the Schloss, his increasing bodily infirmities, his fainting fits, and other intimations of mortality reminded his entourage that the end could not be far away. Moreover, in view of Bismarck's demonstrative preference for attaching Prince Wilhelm rather than the heir-apparent Friedrich to his schemes, made wider circles of Germans wonder whether in the next reign Prussia would be 'germanised' in accordance with Friedrich's sympathies with national liberalism, or Germany 'prussianised' in continuation of Wilhelm I's anti-parliamentarian military idolatry which in 1862 had brought Bismarck into power. Bismarck increasingly inclined towards altering the constitution of 1871, if necessary by force, in order to smash universal suffrage and erect new safeguards against parliamentary supremacy.

On 16th March 1888 the old Emperor died and Friedrich, at long last, became the new Kaiser.

It must, therefore, have come as an unpleasant surprise to the Iron Chancellor that the problem of Germany's immediate future, of the nature of the new reign, came to be decided not by his statecraft, but by providential intervention beyond even his control. Crown Prince Friedrich contracted a throat infection which after a lengthy period of diagnostic uncertainty turned out to be cancer. The first symptoms were observed during March 1887.

Cancer, which thirteen years later was also to carry off the Empress Friedrich, is a mysterious disease. One of the greatest living English experts in cancer research opened an address before professional colleagues in 1966 with the words: 'Happy people do not get cancer.' The Emperor and Empress Friedrich's most injurious unhappiness took its malignant grip on them because, as the most profoundly committed political heirs of the Prince Consort and Queen Victoria, they lived in the conviction that they held the solution for all of Germany's problems, promises, and ills in their hands, but lacked the power and were cheated of the opportunity of putting their ideas into practice. Evil, which they saw embodied in the

Right: The funeral cortege of Friedrich III. For many of his generation this was the premature burial of German liberalism

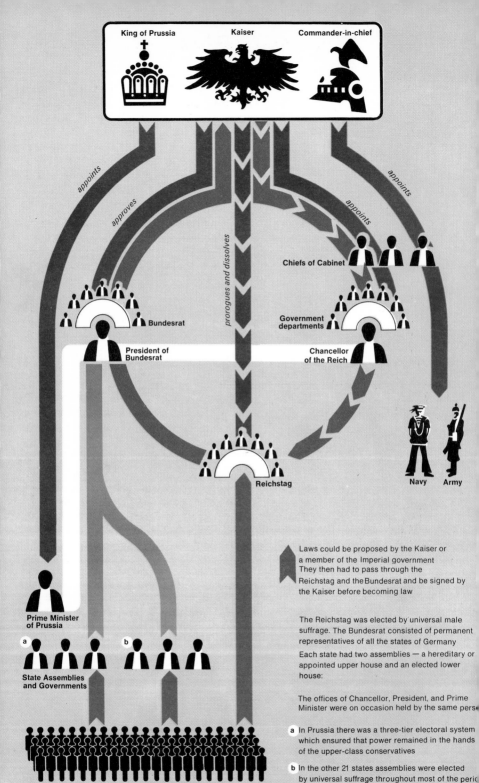

King of Prussia
Kaiser
Commander-in-chief

appoints
approves
appoints
appoints
prorogues and dissolves

Chiefs of Cabinet

Bundesrat

Government
departments

President of
Bundesrat

Chancellor
of the Reich

Navy   Army

Reichstag

Prime Minister
of Prussia

a   b

State Assemblies
and Governments

Electorate

Laws could be proposed by the Kaiser or
a member of the Imperial government
They then had to pass through the
Reichstag and the Bundesrat and be signed by
the Kaiser before becoming law

The Reichstag was elected by universal male
suffrage. The Bundesrat consisted of permanent
representatives of all the states of Germany

Each state had two assemblies — a hereditary or
appointed upper house and an elected lower
house:

The offices of Chancellor, President, and Prime
Minister were on occasion held by the same perso

a In Prussia there was a three-tier electoral system
which ensured that power remained in the hands
of the upper-class conservatives

b In the other 21 states assemblies were elected
by universal suffrage throughout most of the perio

larger-than-life figure of Bismarck, stood in their path and their frustration was total.

With his faith in the irrational magic of Kaiserdom, Friedrich believed in a kind of cultural, scientific, and tribal German imperialism under which German efficiency, industriousness, and inner purity would save the world from materialism, corruption, French decadence, and Russian autocracy. In all these idealistic pursuits he had the vehement and aggressive support of his Vicky who advocated good relations with England, liberalism, and tolerance in a tone of voice that to most of her future subjects sounded neither liberal nor tolerant. In both, self-righteous certainty and their sense of holding a monopoly in political morality and right turned, in the specific context of the realities of the Second German Reich, into incurable disease. It was a tragedy of good intentions, but these at no time included good intentions for their eldest son.

Prince Wilhelm's conduct in the final crisis of his father's life showed that there was little filial piety left in his heart. He expressed concern mainly for the date when his own reign would begin, and the cue was taken by many courtiers and civil servants at the top who jockeyed for position in the new reign, a rat-race of premature gravediggers that gathered momentum and swept the impatient Wilhelm along as the unpredictable nature of Kaiser Friedrich's illness brought conflicting reports from day to day.

Kaiser Friedrich III died on 15th June 1888, at eleven in the morning. Within minutes their Potsdam Palace was surrounded and hermetically sealed off by detachments of the Hussars. No person, and especially no document was allowed to leave the Palais. 'It seemed,' wrote Sir Frederick Ponsonby, 'as if a king had been murdered and his enemy and successor had prepared every detail for taking full possession of his new power.' The Empress Frederick with her three daughters fled to her estate in Brandenburg on 18th June, the anniversary of Waterloo, and Bismarck, heaving a huge sigh of relief, told his family a few days later: 'Well, I've got him in the saddle now.'

Left: Bismarck's masterpiece, the Imperial German constitution

Chapter 4

Getting Rid of Bismarck

The German emperors of the Second Reich held no cere-
monies of coronation and sacred anointment. Instead,
their first appearance before the Reichstag was the
substitute ritual of recognition between Kaiser and
subjects. The reason for this incongruous arrangement
was that according to the Reich constitution of 1871,
the German princes were not the Kaiser's subjects, but
his allies and so could not be expected to wait on the
Emperor disguised in the costume of some antiquated
office. Wilhelm II saw to it that with his version of the
ritual it would become abundantly clear from the start
that a New Era of splendour and glory had dawned upon
the Reich. Within a week of his father's death the Kaiser
had driven through the Brandenburg Gate to the Berlin
Schloss in a carriage drawn by four horses preceded by
outriders and surrounded by gorgeously accoutred
detachments of the *garde du corps*.

A few days later, on 25th June, Reichstag deputies
were summoned to the Schloss where they saw their
young Kaiser surrounded by his German 'allies', the
kings, grand dukes, and margraves of a former Germany.
Old Field-Marshal Moltke stood immediately behind the
pregnant Kaiserin with the baby Crown Prince, 'Little
Willie' of the future, next to him, while Bismarck stood
in front, bowing low over his new master's hand. In a
brief address, the Kaiser promised to 'follow the path
on which my late grandfather won the confidence of his
allies, the love of the German people, and the respect of
foreign countries'. Two days earlier, he had already
taken the oath of allegiance from the armed forces and
told them in a speech that 'I and the army were born for
each other and belong indissolubly together, whether it
will be the will of God to send us calm or storm.' He
reminded them that from the heavens above his Hohenzollern forefathers looked down on him and that eventu-

*Left: Bismarck painted by Lenbach. Born a Junker he was re-
called from a diplomatic post in Paris in 1862 to become Prime
Minister of Prussia and later Chancellor of the Second Reich
which he created and maintained by his ruthless political skill*

53

ally he would have to account to them for the glory and
honour of the army. It was not very long after this that
he referred to Wilhelm I as a sort of honorary member
of the Holy Trinity.

He was in the saddle indeed and meant the world to
take notice. He was twenty-nine on his accession and the
Reich that he had inherited so prematurely had been in
existence for less than two decades. German unification
was regarded, throughout most of the 19th century, as
both inevitable and desirable. In particular, the German
middle classes looked upon it as their inalienable birth
right, and both public opinion in general and the verdict
of historians in particular have come to regard the fact
of unification as a natural and organic development.
Now that over fifty years have elapsed since the last
Kaiser's defeat and abdication, judgement is less unanimous and certain, especially as the Third, or Nazi, Reich
at first looked like a continuation of the militaristic,
economic, and social traditions of its imperial predeces-
sor. Hitler bowing over Hindenburg's hand outside
Potsdam's Garrison Church in 1933 seemed to many the
harbinger of restoration and it was not understood for
many years by the founders of the Third Reich that he
was, on the contrary, a revolutionary of the deepest dye.
Although the promptings of hindsight almost always
produce bad history, it is worth bearing in mind that
thoughtful opinion everywhere—and nowhere more so
than in West Germany today—is reaching the conclusion
that the Bismarck Reich, as founded in 1871, was,
geographically, politically, and constitutionally, a European impossibility that speeded up the end of monarchi-
cal Europe. The Iron Chancellor tends nowadays to be
admired less for his success in founding the Second Reich
than for his gigantic skill in holding it together.

For unification was not followed by unity within the
new frontiers. By making the King of Prussia German
Emperor, a number of German Kingdoms, some with a
Roman Catholic dynasty and properly functioning parlia-
ments, were politically controlled by a Protestant Prussia
ruled on the basis of a three-class suffrage, in which those
who paid the highest taxes automatically possessed the
greatest number of votes, with the result that Prussia,
Germany's largest single state, was permanently ruled
by a rich land-owning and industrialist minority of some
400,000 Conservatives. The Kaiserreich also included
under its suzerainty the three Hanseatic republics of
Hamburg, Bremen, and Lübeck. It included alien minorities to a not inconsiderable degree: Alsace-Lorrainers in
the West, Danes in the North, and Poles in the East. Ger-

Left: The old dog and his new master, Bismarck and Wilhelm II

many was a country 'uniting' within frontiers drawn by the sword people who for long had lived under contrasting degrees of freedom and widely differing social standards, cultures, and electoral laws.

Politically, the Reich that Wilhelm II surveyed from his saddle was represented, in the first Reichstag of his reign (elected in 1890), by 93 Conservatives, 42 National Liberals, 76 Progressives, 106 Centre, 35 Social Democrats; the Poles, Danes, Alsace-Lorrainers, and Hanoverians held between them 38 seats, and the anti-Semitic party five. 'Poles, Hanoverians, Frenchmen, Danes, Social Democrats —' Bismarck had said, 'I regard them all as aliens, and their treatment is a matter of war.' The Kaiser, in his weaker way, took over this sentiment, especially towards the 'alien' Social Democrats. He pursued them with the most venomous *verbal* violence, while towards the Roman Catholics who had been the target of Bismarck's most savage oppression in the period of the *Kulturkampf,* the Kaiser showed an often astonishing tolerance and sympathy.

One is therefore tempted to feel that from its beginning the Second Reich always needed enemies to justify its illogical power structure and internal contradictions. Since Wilhelm II's accession, the 'nightmare of alliances' expressed not only fear of a hostile understanding between two or more foreign countries, but also the realisation that unless there was some external 'threat' south German Catholics, the foreign minorities, and Hanoverian separatists, even the Junkers and traditional Conservatives east of the Elbe who cared nothing for the Reich, might get together with the Catholics of France, Austria, and Poland to escape from Imperial control.

But in that case how was the Second Reich held together? Here we reach perhaps the most important part of the legacy that Bismarck and his system handed over to the young Kaiser. The only national experience shared by all Germans, of whatever social or geographical origin, was service in the armed forces. The military education of all Germans had been in the hands of Prussian officers and drill-sergeants since 1866. Under the various treaties Bismarck had concluded with Prussia's German enemies after the brief war with Austria and the victory at Königgrätz, far-reaching measures of co-ordination had

Top: *Two comments on Bismarck's battles on the home front. He furiously attacks the harmless ladybirds (the Catholic Church) while ignoring the deadly Colorado beetles (liberals and Social Democrats), and he vainly tries to keep down the Social Democrat jack-in-the-box — in spite of his persecution this was to become the most numerous party in the Reichstag.*
Bottom: *The Iron Chancellor with members of the Bundesrat*

been achieved between the Prussian army system and that of the once independent kingdoms of the south. In that sense, those more easy-going lands south of the Main had, after 1866, become Prussian-occupied territories. The Prussian concept of *Obrigkeit* (obedience and docility towards authority) seeped into the character of the new recruits as they were being taught the principal Prussian army virtue of *Kadavergehorsam,* the automatic submission of the mindless body to the degrading and dehumanising tenets of military discipline and drill.

Compulsory military service, the common denominator for Germans of the Second Reich, usually lasted for three years. Sons of what came to be called the 'educated' classes were allowed to serve for one year only to become officers of the Reserve, but whether active or reserve officer, these men in uniform formed in Berlin no less than in countless garrison towns in all parts of Germany the social summit as the representatives of the Kaiser who, as Germany's All-Highest War Lord, was the embodiment of the Reich's military prowess. So far as the army was concerned, the German Eagle, as we saw (page 44) had three heads, the Chief of the Kaiser's Military Cabinet, the Chief of the General Staff, and the Minister of War. Through the Military Cabinet which in the best 18th-century tradition was part of the Imperial Court and not of the official government, the Kaiser had the power of appointing or promoting all officers of the Prussian army. Equally part of his Court, was the Civil Cabinet who advised him on the appointment of chancellors, secretaries of state, the Prussian ministers, and higher civil servants. One of Wilhelm II's rare innovations was that he joined a Naval Cabinet to the other two groups of personal advisers through which all questions of naval policy and personnel were regulated, in many cases before the Chancellor and other responsible ministers had been consulted.

Through these irresponsible institutions, real and direct power had always been in the hands of the Kings of Prussia. As since 1871 the King of Prussia as German Kaiser was also the President of the German Bund, the league of allied and associated German princes, his influence reached deeply into the constitutional life of these lesser monarchies which were, if we include both lines of the house of Reuss, twenty-one in number. Since chancellors, ministers, and other servants of state and Reich remained in office only as long as the Kaiser's favour upheld them, the King/Kaiser's influence on legislation was strong and often decisive. Again, from the beginning, Wilhelm II made it abundantly clear that he

Left: 'Dropping the pilot.' Punch's *comment on Bismarck's fall*

had no intention of allowing his powers, rights, and prerogatives to be curtailed and lessened. It is therefore not surprising that the first clash which this young power-conscious monarch had to fight out was with the Chancellor whom he had not appointed, Bismarck.

While the details of the conflict between Kaiser and Chancellor are complex and often confusing, the basic issue is perfectly simple and clear: was the real power to be in the hands of the Chancellor or the Kaiser? Who was to be the ruler and who the ornament? Wilhelm I had been an ornamental Kaiser (though, of course, a very stubborn King of Prussia), but Wilhelm II, taking his powers literally, intended to be a ruler who ruled. It is usually said of the German Constitution of 1871 that it was tailored by Bismarck according to his own measurements of stature and power. Wilhelm II wished it to fit his own lofty ideas. The Reichstag elections of February 1890 brought into the open the power-rivalry between Kaiser and Bismarck both of whom had manifestly taken up positions from which neither could retreat without the most damaging loss of face.

Following the advice of his personal entourage, the Kaiser expressed on more than one occasion his support for the majority in the Reichstag before the elections which consisted in a block formed by the National Liberals and the Free, or moderate, Conservatives. Equally publicly Bismarck came out in support of a new combination to be formed by the Ultra-Conservatives and the Catholic Centre Party. The Chancellor was all set to smash the parties who since his accession had the Kaiser's avowed confidence and split the Conservatives, his intention being to prove himself once more to be the indispensable man in the political chaos that could be expected to follow from this radical change of political direction. That acts of violence — intervention by the military? a coup d'état against hostile parties in the Reichstag? — might well be part of Bismarck's programme was suspected by a good many people at the time, but it is hard to be certain. That he wanted to create a situation which would have reduced the Kaiser to total dependence on the Chancellor, became clear beyond any possibility of doubt, since Bismarck expressed this in a number of provocative and highly insubordinate actions.

Whether or not the Kaiser, by dismissing Bismarck, saved Germany from bloodshed and violent strife, we need feel no doubt that it was Bismarck's unquenchable thirst for effective power in the Reich he had created that forced the Kaiser to part company with his grandfather's most famous servant. The Kaiser had not acted hastily, impulsively or without due reflection on this occasion, but had often consulted intelligent leaders of

the moderate Conservatives as well as the members of his personal circle. The latter lavishly used strong doses of flattery – a General close to Waldersee told him that Frederick would never have been called 'the Great' if he had had a Minister like Bismarck at his side – to keep the young Kaiser on his anti-Bismarck course.

The final break

The elections produced a victory of the parties backed by Bismarck and a heavy defeat of those backed by the Kaiser. A disagreeable scene took place between Kaiser and Chancellor on 15th March, during which the Kaiser at one time expected the old man to fling an inkstand at him. Bismarck's letter of resignation was received and accepted five days later, but the Kaiser thought it more politic not to publish it. Instead, he let it be known that he regretfully accepted the old Chancellor's resignation tendered for reasons of health, created him Duke of Lauenburg and offered a large monetary gift. Bismarck disdainfully refused the money and said that he might use the title when travelling incognito. He retired to his estate at Friedrichsruh near Hamburg and henceforth became the most formidable member of the opposition to the Reich he had created.

Bismarck's abrupt dismissal reveals that the whole development of the Second Reich went forward not in an orderly process of continuity, but in a series of violent tremors and shocks that seem symptomatic of the Reich's intrinsic insecurity and lack of political coherence. Earlier changes, for example the change-over from Free Trade to Protectionism between 1876 and 1879, had been worked by Bismarck when old Kaiser Wilhelm I was still in his Palace, old Moltke at the head of the army and Bismarck himself directing the affairs of Germany and Europe from his Palais in the Wilhelmstrasse. Although the year 1879 was called by some politicians 'the second founding of the Reich', it had not touched public opinion with anything like the shock-effect produced by the old Chancellor's dismissal in 1890. Two years earlier, two Kaisers had died within three months of each other and a whole generation had been passed over with the death of Friedrich III. Would the young new Kaiser ever find the men to guide and advise him in the way Bismarck, Moltke, and their generation had guided the unambitious old Kaiser? Wilhelm II solved the problem by acting as his own Bismarck and at no time in his reign was he to find the statesman who had the courage and the vision to guide him along the prosaic paths of modern monarchy. The Bismarck system had not bred such men.

Left: The aged Bismarck comes to visit the Kaiser in 1894

Chapter 5
The Summit of the German Volcano

Wilhelm II's reign was determined throughout the thirty years of its duration by the unpredictable interplay between character and office, the flaws and weaknesses of his personal nature, and the extensive and comprehensive powers that were his under the constitution. At the same time, he was a man of conspicuous gifts and talents, possessing a quick rather than original mind, a natural aptitude to absorb the intricacies of any problem submitted to him, an excellent memory, and, when he chose to exercise it, a charm of manner and winning courtesy that enchanted all manner of people.

We might call him a strong personality, but a weak character. His nervous system, the normal development of his mind and soul, had been badly damaged since birth and childhood. He was a man without patience and powers of steady application, although he made strenuous efforts from time to time to cultivate his mind. His friendship with Eulenburg took him into the fields, such as they were, of music and poetry, the lectures which he asked Walter Rathenau to give him privately in his study temporarily filled his mind with information on Europe's economic, industrial, and financial realities, and other examples could be quoted of his searching in the fields of science, archaeology, and academic erudition for intellectual stimulus and study.

The Kaiser's health was never good or strong, and there was a distinct trait of the hypochondriac in his make-up. His temper was uncertain and incalculable and with his unbalanced nervous system he was, at all times in his reign, at the mercy of his temperamental moods and whims to an extent that lends a touch of accuracy to the much-used cliché of 'the personal rule of Wilhelm II'. This is an exaggeration and over-simplification, even under the conditions of the Second Reich. Yet, in so far as the great powers which fell into his lap after Bismarck's dismissal allowed him to let his temper fly in its neurotic vehemence, his nervous frailty became a personal-political factor of some consequence.

Left: A French cartoon typifies the European view of Wilhelm

63

Yet it would not be entirely accurate to say that he was just an immature man with a quick temper. Within the same temperamental disposition there lived a real urge for conciliation, a desire to bring the warring factions of his fatherland, and later the rival powers of the world, closer together on a basis of peace and understanding. We must, therefore, regard him as a man who, deeply divided in his inner self, had been through no fault of his own propelled into his high and powerful position before he was ready, and so took the solution of escaping from his conflicts, his feelings of inadequacy, insecurity, and lack of nervous (as well as physical) balance by turning himself into the shining, noisy, and oratorically forceful representative of Germany's claims for her place in the sun, a sort of eagle-helmeted Lohengrin whose holy grail was German *Weltpolitik*. His mild and pleasant features now became disfigured with that famous moustache of the upturned ends which some people thought was in itself a declaration of war.

'If you are the summit of a volcano,' wrote Sir Winston Churchill in his essay on the Kaiser, 'the least you can do is to smoke. So he smoked, a pillar of cloud by day and the gleam of fire by night, to all who gazed from afar; and slowly and surely these perturbed observers gathered and joined themselves together for mutual protection.' Earlier in the same essay we read that if the Kaiser had talked peace from his summit, his subjects, in the assertive and outward-looking atmosphere of the Second Reich, would have exclaimed: 'We have a weakling on the throne. Our War Lord is a pacifist. Is this new-arrived, late-arrived German Empire with all its tremendous and expanding forces to be led by a president of the Young Men's Christian Association?' The Kaiser's speeches – 406 were recorded in the first twelve years of his reign – were belligerent, boastful, threatening, and, one must add, often downright silly; his actions, from the dismissal of war-at-any-price General von Waldersee in 1891 over the two Moroccan crises of 1905 and 1911, to some point, not easily determined, in his jubilee year 1913, expressed his desire for European peace. He talked war, he acted peace; the shades and details of German politics and European complications were beyond the scope of his understanding. He was, almost to the last, a man without self-knowledge or judgment of the psychology of other people and other countries. Until the war he did not want broke out in 1914, he was unclear in his own mind about the distinction between a constitutional and an autocratic monarch, and so he was always both.

Left: Wish fulfilment. The Kaiser as Frederick the Great
Far left: The grandson of Queen Victoria in Stewart tartan

The divided Reich

The Chancellors whom the Kaiser called in between Bismarck's dismissal and the outbreak of war were four in number: General von Caprivi, Prince von Hohenlohe, Bülow, and Bethmann Hollweg. With the exception of the first-named, these men were also Prime Ministers of Prussia and, as such, presided over the Prussian Ministry of State. This dualism meant that, whereas as Chancellors of the Reich they had to pursue a modified liberal policy, as Prussian Prime Ministers they were faced with a permanent majority of landowners, bureaucrats, and industrialists who in all cases put their own interests above those of the Reich as a whole.

Prussia was not only the Second Reich's biggest, but also most separatist country. The area of possible conflicts between Prussia and Reich was therefore wide, as Caprivi, Bismarck's immediate successor, very soon found out. 'Germany,' he said, 'must either export people or goods,' and by a determined policy of lowering the tariff barriers between Germany and its European customers and suppliers, he stimulated the export trade and marketing abroad. Since 1848, the Germans had been a nation of emigrants, but thanks to Caprivi's liberalising reforms this 'export of people' dwindled to a trickle and unemployment figures were greatly reduced. Most industrialists as well as the various chambers of commerce throughout the Reich welcomed Caprivi's measures. Not so, however, Prussian landowners who felt threatened by the import of cheap wheat and grain with its resultant fall in the price of bread and other agricultural commodities. They organised a number of extra-parliamentary pressure groups and went to the country in an anti-Caprivi propaganda campaign of exceptional virulence and vulgarity until, as one of the agriculturist leaders remarked, 'we are heard at the steps of the throne'.

In a speech given at Königsberg in September 1894, the Kaiser came out in support of his Chancellor. At a sumptuous banquet to which landowners East of the Elbe, heads of historic families and the high military and bureaucratic dignitaries of the region had been summoned, he told his audience that it was unnatural for true Prussians to form an opposition to their king. Instead, they should give him their support in the fight against those who were undermining 'the fundaments of our political and social life'. He ended with a stirring call to arms: 'Forward in the fight for religion, morality, and order against the parties of revolution *(Umsturz).*'

Left from top: Chancellors of the Reich: Caprivi 1890-94; Hohenlohe 1894-1900; Bülow 1900-04; Bethmann Hollweg 1904-07. Far left: Members of the Reichstag work in the library

If he thus reproached the leaders of Prussia for their opposition to his Chancellor, he endeavoured to divert their attention from their agricultural protectionism to the necessity of fighting the Progressive and Socialist enemy at home. The Conservatives took him at his word and demanded stringent new laws against the parties of the left. If hitherto the Kaiser had been under fire from his faithful Prussian Conservatives who at Court and in social life were closer to him than any other class of subjects, he was now attacked by those parties in the Reich that viewed the proposed legislation against the left with the gravest misgivings. In September, Caprivi felt secure in the success of his commercial policy which, in his own way, the Kaiser had backed by autocratically prohibiting opposition, even from Prussians. But on 25th October 1894, he was summoned to Potsdam and in an audience lasting one minute, dismissed by the Kaiser who told him: 'My nerves cannot stand it any more, I must dismiss you.'

With these words, Wilhelm II gave voice to the King of Prussia and silenced the German Emperor. He spoke as the head of the conservatives and ignored the inherent needs of the bourgeois and liberal Reich. Although never approving of Pan-German alarums and artificially engendered patriotism, he became, after Caprivi's dismissal, far more closely identified, in the sphere of Court and private life, with the unyielding conservatives of his country's society.

We need not concern ourselves with Caprivi's successor, Prince von Hohenlohe, a civilised Bavarian aristocrat who at seventy-five had reached the age of inaction and was, on the whole, content to leave well alone. He was also, for one reason and another, in a state of financial dependence on the Kaiser and counted for little on that fierce battlefield that was German politics. We may just note that by the time he arrived in his high office, naval affairs had been finally taken out of the hands of the army and given to professional sailors. Admiral von Tirpitz became Secretary of State of the Naval Office in 1897 and the Kaiser's old idea of putting army and fleet on a basis of equality and social parity was realised.

Nor did Hohenlohe bring any changes into the Caprivi system of diminished protectionism, and German commerce and trade relations continued to prosper in European and world markets. With this global expansionism went a dynamic upsurge of prosperity at home, making the rich richer and the poor more deprived than ever, but this was, of course, not a specifically German problem. At the same time, Germany's social structure was

Right: *Fantasy and back to normal; the Kaiser and Kaiserin*

marked, more so than elsewhere, by a certain lack of mobility, domestic tolerance, and ease. The nation remained divided into its various groups and castes, separated one from the other by the most rigid and stiff lines of demarcation and social discrimination. The Wilhelminian system of dispensing honours, titles, and decorations accentuated these divisions. Even when, as happened so often, noble Junker families allowed the daughters, and sometimes sons, of industrial and commercial magnates to marry into their once exclusive families for financial reasons, it signified only that the upper reaches of the bourgeoisie became more Prussian than the Junkers themselves.

A rebellion against philistinism

Despite the rigidity and stiffness of German social and cultural life, the Second Reich saw the birth of a number of lively, non-conformist, and deviationist minority movements in the educational, literary, and artistic spheres which rebelled against the massive philistinism and assertive patriotism of the social establishment. From 1894 onwards, a number of independent private boarding schools were founded in all parts of the German countryside in opposition to the state-run schools where near-military discipline and an authoritarian teaching system were the rule. 'Let us not sell youth's birthright for a mess of pottage called middle-class utility,' said one of the founders of these new school communities, expressing an urge for greater freedom and the cult of individuality, that was felt vividly among the younger generations.

Another minority of gifted deviators in the 1890s conquered such theatres as were not under official control. The Kaiser, in one of his numerous public speeches, had called the stage 'one of my weapons' with which he wanted to fight 'materialism and the un-German type of art'. His favourite dramatist was a man called Ernst von Wildenbruch, by coincidence himself a Hohenzollern of illegitimate origins. Wildenbruch wrote historical dramas and pageants filled with massive and monumental patriotism. A contemporary diarist had thought of this Court dramatist and his latest play on the Emperor Henry IV that 'German-national sentimentality sounds strange on the lips of Henry IV and from time to time one seems to listen, not to him, but to an edict or speech by His present Majesty'. During a later performance, the students of Berlin University intended to boo and whistle the piece off the stage, but desisted because Their Majesties were present in the Imperial box.

Left: 'Germania', the spirit of Imperial Germany—a typical example of official culture from a play sponsored by the Kaiser

Un-German materialism, on the other hand, was the Kaiser's allusion to the great dramatist Gerhart Hauptmann, whose play *Die Weber (The Weavers)* had its first performance in 1892. In a sense, this was also a historical drama, for it dealt with the rising of the starving weavers of Silesia in 1844, but the underlying attack on social suffering and injustice shot through with real compassion for the hopeless fate of the very poor was not lost on the audience, especially as the drama was written in a starkly naturalistic idiom that left very little to the imagination. The police and judiciary authorities immediately subjected author and play to a record number of prosecutions and court cases, accusing Hauptmann of revolutionary intent against the order in state and society, of being an *Umsturzdichter,* a prophet of destruction. Much to his honour, he wrote a number of further social dramas which with their poetic realism and humour changed the face of the German theatre overnight.

When a Berlin literary jury awarded the annual Schiller prize (6,000 marks and a gold medal) to Hauptmann, the Kaiser forbade this and gave reward and medal to his distant cousin Wildenbruch. The chairman of the jury thereupon resigned, giving his reasons in public. We can only conclude that it must have come as a terrible blow to the Kaiser when in 1912 Hauptmann received the Nobel Prize for Literature.

Statistics covering the whole period of the Second Reich show that internationally the German language was learned and studied by more people than at any other time in modern history. From the United States over the universities of Europe to the Far East, German, the language of success, held the first place in the study of foreign languages. This is not surprising in view of the fact that German commercial firms were penetrating the markets in all parts of the world, that German architects, engineers, and industrialists built railways, factories, harbour installations, and housing estates in all parts of the world. Some foreign countries, especially Japan, Turkey, and to a limited extent China, sent military missions to Berlin to study the technique of victory and success, and in the practical field the German language had, after 1870, become a must.

Top right: *Paternalism in industry. Workers' houses built by Krupp. The great industrial companies took good care of their workers—providing pensions, sickness benefits, and homes— but only if they were not socialists or trade union members.*
Bottom right: *Paternalism in education. The foundation is laid for Germany's leadership in the sciences. State schools under the Second Reich were among the most advanced in Europe*

On the literary scene, a number of exceptionally gifted writers of prose and poetry made their debut, again outside the official mode. Thomas Mann, Stefan George, Rainer Maria Rilke, and others rescued the German language—the language of the schoolmaster and the sergeant-major, said Nietzsche in the 1880s—from the servitude into which it had so glaringly fallen since the days of Goethe and the great Romantics. In the musical field, the Kaiser, much to his discomfiture, had to witness the triumphs, national and international, of Richard Strauss, the acme of his own musical taste being the Norwegian composer Edvard Grieg. In the visual arts, among the Kaiser's principal favourites was Adolph von Menzel, a specialist in costume pieces on Frederick the Great and his Court, the exact reproduction of which gave the Kaiser many an opportunity for giving Frederician fancy-dress parties at Sans-souci. Great painting flourished outside the official sphere and its most talented masters, among whom we might mention the young Oskar Kokoschka, having seceded from the academic establishment, exhibited in the annual 'secessionist' salon. Finally, in 1911 a young architect called Walter Gropius achieved a memorable breakthrough by building a factory in the austere cubic outline enlivened with huge areas of glass that became the model for the new style of factory architecture in the years to come. In 1915 the Grand Duke of Saxe-Weimar put Gropius in charge of the Saxon Academy of Arts and Crafts and so unconsciously laid the foundation of what was to become the Bauhaus.

'Art of the gutter'

In so far as the Kaiser was aware of these many independent movements bubbling over with the spirit of innovation, originality, and change, he was apt to bundle them all together in the hated category of 'un-German materialism' or 'art of the gutter'. When at the end of 1901 he unveiled the final group of statuary in Berlin's Tiergarten, his 'Victory Alley' consisting of monuments to his Hohenzollern ancestors, however obscure and forgettable, at the ensuing banquet he addressed the sculptors involved in this hideous Imperial pet-project:

'Art which transgresses the laws and limits laid down by me can no longer be called art . . . To us Germans mankind's great ideals have become our lasting possession, while to other nations they have been more or less lost. . . . When Art, as happens so frequently these days, does

Right: Provincial Germany, a street scene in the old part of Hamburg. Top right: The honours system turns the Red Flag into the Imperial Banner. A comment on the greed for decorations. Bottom right: The Kaiser cuts his chancellor down to size

nothing but make misery more miserable still, it commits a sin against the German people.'

How seriously did his people take the Kaiser? When in 1890 the Kaiser, in an order of the day, announced that aristocracy of birth was no longer enough but must be joined by a new aristocracy of the soul, a Berlin newsboy was heard to shout: 'Kaiser's latest Easter present! All aristocracy forbidden, only aristocracy of the soul allowed.' They called him the Reisekaiser, the travelling Emperor, since in the first decade of his reign he averaged nearly two hundred days per year travelling on official business or private recreation in his famous special train. 'I know they call me Reisekaiser,' he once told another accepted writer, the folksy and exceedingly banal Bavarian Ludwig Ganghofer, 'but this I have always taken very lightly.' There is no question of the Kaiser not having a sense of humour, but at first satirists and humorous critics of the All-Highest person and his public conduct did not always get off lightly.

It has been estimated that up to 1906 between five and six hundred trials for *lèse-majesté* were held in Germany. When in 1906 a French cartoonist published a collection of Kaiser caricatures in a volume entitled *Lui*, the Kaiser gave personal instructions to allow the work to be imported without any obstacles. In the following year, he insisted in a personal letter to the minister of justice that only those offenders against the *lèse-majesté* laws who could be proved to have acted from evil intent and not from ignorance, lack of reflection, and impulsiveness should be punished, after which these persecutions were greatly reduced in number.

'I have no time for ruling,' was another Berlin witticism caused by the Kaiser's travel-crazy restlessness. When, with every show of reluctance, he settled down to a stint of governmental work, he preferred working with, and through, the heads of his three private cabinets, Military, Civil, and Naval, reducing to the unavoidable minimum systematic work with the Chancellor and secretaries of state who under the constitution had one foot in the, to him, pernicious Reichstag and other parliamentary institutions. Holstein, the first one-time supporter to be disillusioned by the young Kaiser's 'comic opera government', even thought that Wilhelm and the three chiefs of cabinet were ruling *against* the constitutional organs of government. He said so in a letter to Philipp Eulenburg who himself expressed grave doubts concerning the eventual synthesis 'between Prussian blood and south German liberalism — I fear that only a successful war would give the Kaiser the prestige he needs in his fight against parliamentary government'.

Holstein was inclined to agree but added: 'In a war of aggression we would have to expect a number of strange surprises . . . and there is at present no reason for a defensive war since nobody wants to do anything against us. . . .' He went on to accuse Eulenburg of having changed from 'a simple Royalist to a Court-Conservative of the new dispensation' and followed this up with the prophetic remark that while Eulenburg was thinking only of the Kaiser, he, Holstein, was thinking of the dynasty's future which the Kaiser was endangering by wastefully living off 'Royalist capital' which his son and 'probably he himself will sadly miss in a few years'. This correspondence took place late in 1894.

The fantasy of Prussianism

If at the summit of Germany's social pyramid the Kaiser was indeed surrounded by 'Court Conservatives', the political representatives of this party in the country were extremely treacherous allies for the head of the Reich.

In 1903 the Pan-German Association, another of those extra-parliamentary pressure groups, held a mass meeting addressed by one of its founders, Justizrat Heinrich Class, on the theme 'Changes in Germany's world position since 1890'. Needless to say, these changes had all been for the worse, and it was the Kaiser's fault. That speech, printed as a pamphlet, sold some 60,000 copies and Class said complacently that meeting and pamphlet between them had laid the foundation to 'a determined and comprehensive national opposition'.

In other words, if to his un-Prussian-minded subjects the Kaiser's rule went too far in the direction of autocracy and irresponsibility, it did not go far enough for those of the traditional Prussian faith. Prussianism, of course, was never a matter of geography confined to those born between the Elbe and the Russian frontier, it was rather a form of upper-class religion and military allegiance that acted as a converting agent in many parts of the Reich. Yet, since German unification, Prussian traditionalism had become a sponsored fantasy. The social structure of the German army exemplifies the decline of the privileged supremacy of the Prussian system protected by the shield of a strong monarchy. By 1914, the German peacetime army stood at a strength of 760,905 NCOs and men. They were led by an officer corps that was seventy per cent bourgeois while the percentage of noble generals and colonels had sunk from eighty to fifty-two

Left: 'Libertas Academica' — a cartoon commenting on the fact that intellectuals in the Second Reich found it difficult to avoid being shackled by the anti-democratic ideals of the Prussian state

per cent. As we have seen, the Junker class found in political Conservativism a method to arrest its threatened decline, while the middle classes with their new economic power and wealth saved the Junker from extinction in that alliance of aristocratic 'von's' and bourgeois 'funds' so important to the social scene of the Second Reich. The bourgeoisie, like the Junkers, continued to look upwards to Kaiser and Court as the prestigious prop for their way of life and guarantee for its continuance. Politically, on the other hand, the Conservatives regarded themselves as members of the opposition and would rather let the Reich go smash than make the smallest concession touching on their privileges and waning power.

Philipp Eulenburg, essentially a man of moderation and temperate opinions, during the Caprivi crisis told the Kaiser that the Chancellor he needed had to be 'a man who is neither conservative nor liberal, neither ultra-montane nor progressive, neither ritualist nor atheist...', an identikit sketch that held out little hope of finding so elusive a personage. Eulenburg also thought that 'the somewhat worn phrase of the king having to stand above the parties means, when translated into practical terms, nothing more than that he must depend on the middle parties'. Again a perfectly sensible prescription except for the difficulty that the middle parties between them were unable to unite in a practicable political alliance.

Right: Guards recruits march through the streets of Berlin

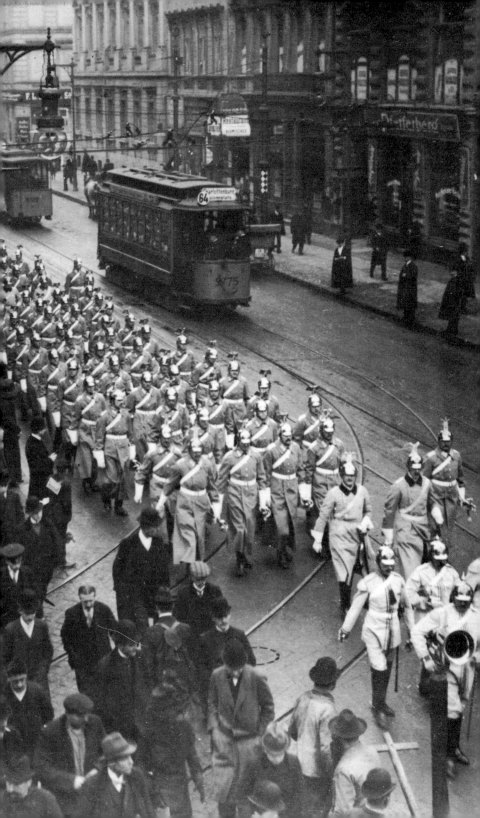

Flowers in a cultural desert

As with society in the Second Reich, all official cultural activity bore the stamp of conformity to standards set by the Kaiser (**below** at an exhibition). In contrast to his intelligent support of science, his attempts to mould the nation's taste in the arts gave German culture a monumental and false facade. Yet the Reich did see a flowering of works of lasting genius — the social realism of dramatists like Gerhardt Hauptmann and Hermann Sudermann nightly filled Berlin's private theatres; men like Thomas Mann, Rainer Maria Rilke, and Stefan George entered the world of literature as it were behind the Kaiser's back. Full freedom of artistic expression existed in the Second Reich and despite official disapproval, a real creative artist in any field could find an audience among large sections of the Kaiser's subjects. **Right:** Richard Wagner, one of the giants of German music whom the Kaiser called a 'cheap little conductor'. **Far right:** Two milestones in modern literature — the covers of Hauptmann's *Die Weber* and Thomas Mann's *Buddenbrooks*

DIE·W[E]BER

HAUPTMANN

Thomas Mann

Buddenbrooks

Berlin
S. Fischer, Verlag.

Rise in German Trade Union Membership

1913 1910 1905 1900 1896 1891

344,000
409,000
851,000
1,650,000
2,435,000
3,024,000

North Sea

Kiel Canal
Lübeck
Hamburg
Bremen
Ems-Weser Canal
Hanover
O
O
Weser-Elbe Canal
Berlin
L
L
Dortmund-Ems Canal
C
Mittelland Canal
L
L
L
I
I
P
P
L
Halle
L L L L L L
L L L L L L L L
Rhine River
Duisburg
Düsseldorf
C C
C
C C C
Dortmund
Essen
Wuppertal
L L
L
I
I
I I
Cologne
I
I
Leipzig
L L
L L
L L
L
Dresden
C
Chemnitz
C C
P
Wiesbaden
Frankfurt
Saarbrücken
C C
C C C C
C C
I I
Mannheim
Nürnberg
I
Rhine River
Stuttgart
I
I
Munich
Rhine River
L L
L
L

◇ Industrial Areas
C Coal
L Lignite
I Iron Ore Deposits
P Potash
O Oilfields

| 25 | 50 | 75 | 100 | MLS
| 50 | 100 | 150 | KMS

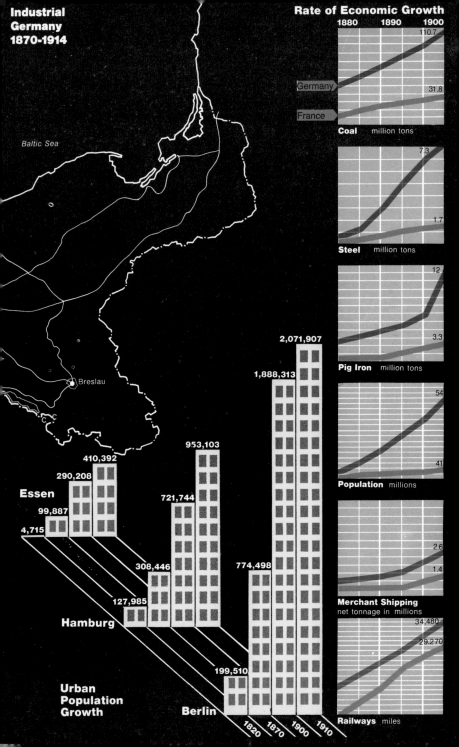

Industrial Germany 1870-1914

Baltic Sea

Breslau

Rate of Economic Growth

1880　1890　1900

Germany
France

Coal　million tons
110.7
31.8

Steel　million tons
7.3
1.7

Pig Iron　million tons
12
3.3

Population　millions
54
41

Merchant Shipping
net tonnage in millions
2.6
1.4

Railways　miles
34,480
29,270

Urban Population Growth

Essen
4,715
99,887
290,208
410,392

Hamburg
127,985
308,446
721,744
953,103

Berlin
199,510
774,498
1,888,313
2,071,907

1820　1870　1900　1910

Chapter 6
Foreign Relations

How did that semi-liberalistic, paternalist, and militaristic anarchy called the Second Reich stand in Europe and the world? When Holstein wrote in 1894 that there was nobody who harboured any hostile designs against Germany, he showed himself to be remarkably free from that persecution complex and haunting fear of being surrounded by a world of enemies that was an integral part of the psychological make-up of all Germans. The Royal Navy, for example, was always being suspected of planning the total destruction of the inferior German fleet, as long as it remained inferior. Russia, the colossus from which Germany was separated by no natural frontier, was another source of nightmare apprehensions, especially when after her defeat in the Japanese war she turned away from the east to become once again a major European power. A decade before then, the Third French Republic and Tsarist Russia had formed their alliance, and in the seventh year of the Kaiser's reign the world was treated to the spectacle of the Tsar, Nicholas II, receiving the President of the French Republic on the quai-side at Kronstadt and baring his head as the band struck up the anthem of the Revolution, the *Marseillaise*. Germany did not, after the Kaiser's accession, renew the secret treaty with Russia which Bismarck, as a covering bet, had concluded under the name of the Reinsurance Treaty. Bismarck regarded this diplomatic coup as a protection for Germany in the event of either Russia or Austria starting an aggressive war against the other in connection with their conflicting interests in the Balkans — a conflict that Bismarck himself had made so probable by turning Austria into a Balkan power instead of a Germanic one and by providing a strong motive for aggression from either side by putting Bosnia under Austrian *de facto* rule.

Left: 'The power of the press.' A Simplicissimus cartoon shows peaceful Germany being lulled to sleep by his newspaper while the 'European' beasts gather around him. They include the bear of Russia, the lion of Great Britain, and the cockerel of France. Fear of encirclement was very widespread in Germany

85

Holstein, in his backroom at the Wilhelmstrasse, had been a driving force behind the 'away from Russia' turn with all its anti-Bismarckian implications. Towards France, on the contrary, he firmly maintained the Bismarckian line of keeping the Republic isolated and humbled. Germany and France clashed twice over the Moroccan question, first in 1905 while Holstein was still in office, and again in 1911 when he was dead. Germany's late-arrived Imperialism had been defined in a famous speech by Chancellor von Bülow who said that while she wanted to put nobody into the shade, Germany demanded her place in the sun. The Kaiser's definition had been that henceforth no major decisions in colonial questions and conflicts must be reached without Germany having her decisive say in it. Otherwise he viewed the possibility of armed conflict entirely as a personalising dynast. Let him only meet his cousin 'Nicky' and all German-Russian tensions would disappear like a dream at dawn, and for years he yearned for an opportunity of paying a state visit to France.

Tsar Nicholas II, ten years younger than the Kaiser, was a feeble, banal, and retiring man, stubborn in character and protectively armoured with an irreducible faith in his autocratic powers. He had grown up under the strong anti-German influence of his father, Alexander III, and married a Princess of Hesse-Darmstadt, a granddaughter of Queen Victoria. They both preferred a life of rustic domesticity away from the semi-barbarous splendour of the Court at St Petersburg and the coarse extravagance of the Russian nobility. Less intelligent and eloquent than the Kaiser, he somewhat helplessly drifted into the part of the recipient of Wilhelm's educational ardour. The Kaiser lectured his younger fellow-autocrat on his sacred duties as absolute ruler and did what he could to steady 'Nicky's' vaccilations. There were even public salutations from 'Willie' as 'The Admiral of the Atlantic' to a 'Nicky' promoted to 'The Admiral of the Pacific' – a source of embarrassment rather than encouragement to the shivering Tsar of All the Russias.

On 24th July 1905 when Russia had just suffered disastrous defeat by Japan and her cities and provinces were in the grip of workers' strikes and peasant disorders, Tsar and Kaiser met on the remote island of Björkö in the Baltic. Wilhelm persuaded the less articulate Nicholas to sign along with him a treaty of 92 ▷

Bottom right: A French cartoonist sees the Kaiser's visit to the Near East as a great variety show – 'Only one performance a day', 'Soldiers half price'. Top right: The Kaiser as the one-man-band of Europe, a comment on his attempts to play every possible role. Right: Part of the entourage of the reluctant traveller rides through the streets of Tangiers in 1905

Le Rire

TOURNÉE GUILLAUME II   15 JOURS EN

TURQUIE, PALESTINE

JÉRUSALEM ET
LES LIEUX SAINTS

VU LES EXIGENCES DE L'ITINÉRAIRE
IL NE SERA DONNÉ QU'UNE
SEULE REPRÉSENTATION DANS CHAQUE
LOCALITÉ

LES MILITAIRES
PAIENT
1/2 PLACE

POUR TOUS RENSEI-
GNEMENTS
S'ADRESSER
AUX
VEBER'S

The social tone
of Imperial Germany

In spite of the rampant Germanic nationalism of the Second Reich abroad, there was little feeling of real political unity within Imperial Germany. Although there was universal suffrage in the elections to the Reichstag, the attitude of the average citizen to his government was one of almost total apathy. He believed in obedience rather than participation, and made his way through life along a strict system which might award him the title of councillor or some other decoration as long as his politics were conformist and his bourgeois morals correct. The habit of discipline was learned in the conscript army, and it was the military which set the social tone for society. **Below:** One of the host of the uniformed civil service—the warden of a river. **Top:** A cartoon on the militarism of civilian life (left) and duelling students (right). **Bottom:** Secure in their status, a group of leading citizens. **Next page:** The bastion of conservative society, the Imperial Court

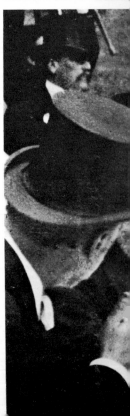

eternal friendship between their two countries, but when the two rulers returned to their respective capitals their governmental advisers were horrified and the treaty of Björkö, jotted down on a scrap of blue writing paper, never came to life. Nevertheless, they continued to exchange letters and visits up to 1913 in the hope of keeping the glamour of unfettered kingship alive in the eyes of the gaping public.

'The creeping malaise of Europe'

The hope of a state visit to France was doomed by the prolonged Franco-German crisis over Morocco, a creeping malaise of which the European body politic was not really freed until November 1911. When in April 1904 the world learned that Lord Lansdowne for Britain and Théophile Delcassé for France had concluded a colonial agreement that became known as the Entente Cordiale, it also learned that in exchange for giving up her claims in Egypt, France had been given a free hand to establish a protectorate over the disintegrating and chaotic kingdom of Morocco. Consequently, the French forthwith put the Sultan under considerable pressure for far-reaching concessions of an administrative and commercial nature. The latter point was particularly obnoxious to Germany, for French colonial protectorates meant protection in the sense of high tariffs, trading monopolies, and the exclusion of competitors. Having from the German point of view quite legitimately thrown a spanner into an Anglo-French accord he did not like, Bülow next proceeded to take a measure that was without any doubt the worst and most fatal blunder of his nine years of chancellorship. He induced an extremely reluctant and furiously objecting Kaiser to visit Tangiers in person during his forthcoming Mediterranean cruise. A full-dress campaign was unleashed in the press, including the Pan-German papers, to the effect that only Germany's All-Highest War Lord could see to it that Germany's true claims and rights were not disdainfully ignored by the French and British, and advice poured in from all sides on Wilhelm urging him to dramatic gesture for the benefit of German prestige and world position.

A few days before the cruise was to start, the Kaiser sent a telegram to Bülow in a final attempt to escape from the demonstration:

Right: The search for Germany's place in the sun. Troops on the Great Wall of China after putting down the Boxer revolt. *Top right:* 'My idea of Africa was very different,' says a German officer as he flees from the natives. *Bottom right:* 'Revenge'. Having been decorated by the Kaiser, a Somali chief gives gold nose rings in return to two of the Imperial princes

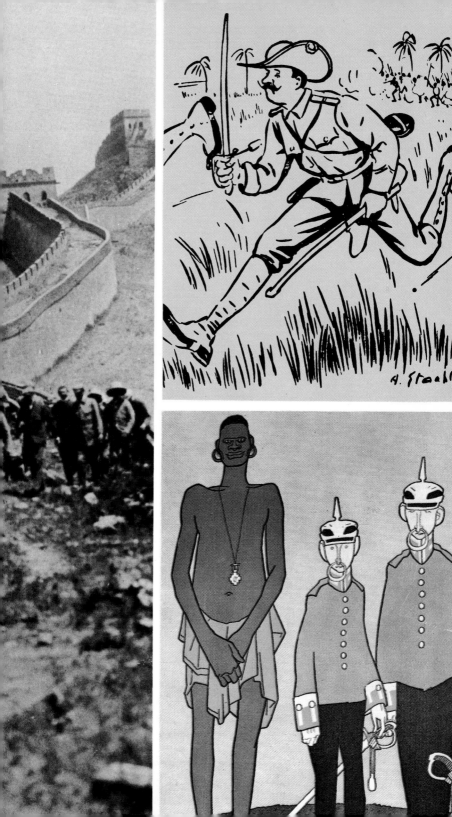

'I see from newspaper reports that German settlers in Morocco and Moroccans are making preparations to over-exploit my visit and play out French against English. Telegrams must be forthwith sent to Tangiers that it is most doubtful that I shall land there, that I am travelling incognito as a tourist and want no audiences or receptions.

Yet land in Tangiers he did, accepting in all constitutional propriety the advice of his Chancellor and Prime Minister. The whole inner falseness of the Second Reich's governmental machinery as well as the Kaiser's inability to face up to strong opposition, were revealed in one fateful flash. Even so, he did what he could to temper the provocative melodrama of the Tangiers landing with reasonable speeches. Calling on the Sultan's representative at Tangiers on 31st March 1905, he described the Sultan mildly enough as the ruler of a free and independent country not subject to any foreign domination, a state of affairs which he intended to support with all his might.

The most fatal consequence of Tangiers was that in the eyes of the British government the *entente,* which had been regarded as a purely Imperial and naval arrangement to put an end to two hundred years of Anglo-French colonial rivalry, now threatened to be extended to Europe itself. Lansdowne, unlike certain vocal sections of British public opinion and the press, saw in the *entente cordiale,* as conceived in 1903-4, no anti-German bias of any sort whatever. Delcassé, a temperamental statesman reared in the great revolutionary tradition of France which the Third Republic had so powerfully revived since Sedan and the redemption of Captain Dreyfus, tended to regard the understanding with England as a first step in the forming of a new grouping of powers that would free France from the German tutelage which had been hanging over her since Napoleon III's defeat at Sedan.

But Delcassé was more popular with public opinion in England than with his colleagues in the government and the majority of deputies at the Palais Bourbon. Nor was his project of a fully-fledged alliance welcomed by the Conservative government in England, shocked and exasperated though Prime Minister Balfour and Lansdowne himself were by the Kaiser's visit to the Sultan's territory. In the end, Delcassé was forced to resign from the Foreign Ministry and his opponent, Pierre Rouvier, who advocated a peaceful understanding with Germany by diplo-

*Left: The warlord in peacetime, directing manoeuvres. **Top left:** Explaining finer military points to the Prince Regent of Bavaria. **Bottom:** 'Food or manoeuvres?' The German farmer is crowded off his land by the demands of the army for space*

matic means, won the day. Early in 1906, an international conference met at Algeciras in Spain, and although Bülow still hoped to undermine the Anglo-French *entente* in the end he had to climb down considerably in the face of an almost unanimous opposition by the other powers, including Germany's ally Italy, and be content with a number of concessions that were more apparent than real. Bülow's Moroccan policy had been a flop, but the Kaiser paid a heavy price. The first Moroccan crisis may be said to have found its finale when Holstein resigned from his post at the Wilhelmstrasse and took the Bismarckian policy of keeping France out of what some people still called the Concert of Europe with him into retirement.

The lasting effect of Bülow's inept and clumsy technique of opening the European debate on a colonial arrangement by pushing the Kaiser into the foreground was that in the countries most closely affected nationalistic patriotism raised its bellicose head higher than ever before. Anglo-German relations in particular were henceforth to be dominated by new pressures and emotional recriminations that the two countries had not known since the days of the Boer War.

Family rivalry

Anglo-German relations, since Wilhelm's accession, had shown the same unstable ups and downs that we have observed in other aspects of the Kaiser's political conduct. So far as these relations were reflected in the personal relationship between Wilhelm and his senior British uncle, Edward VII, they were poisoned from the very beginning. The Kaiser was haunted by an almost hysterical fear of 'outside interference' (by which phrase he invariably meant English politicians) in the affairs of the Reich — a fear of Germany becoming a kind of British satellite and having to ask permission in London before taking any steps in the pursuit of its own interests. Obviously, this kind of obsession reflected, in the Kaiser's case, the story of his childhood and adolescence and so the cheerful and politically impotent figure of Uncle Edward grew in his mind into a sort of Machiavellian ogre dedicated to stunting and strangling German freedom of action.

That Wilhelm's image of his uncle as a hostile super-diplomat was a temperamental fantasy need no longer be stressed. After becoming King in 1901, Edward VII was as inconsistent in the field of Anglo-German relations as was the Kaiser himself — with the difference that

Left: The Kaiser and Edward VII of England going in the same direction for once. Wilhelm was deeply suspicious of his uncle

97

in Edward's case his changing impulses had no influence on the policies of his governments and officials,
whereas in the Kaiser's case, with his greater powers
on paper, his moods and fancies were of consequence
since several important men in his entourage exploited
his fears and suspicions of England and King Edward
to their own ends. Of this Chancellor von Bülow was a
glaring example especially as he used Edward's alleged
intrigues of encirclement as an alibi for his own blunders.

This background must be borne in mind when we recall
the first major Anglo-German crisis of the reign that
followed the Kaiser's famous telegram he sent on 3rd
January 1895 to President Kruger of the Transvaal after
the ignominious Jameson raid on Boer territory. Germany
had important economic interests in South Africa, and
the question whether Britain or Germany should take the
Boer Republic under its 'protection' had already caused
considerable animosity in Berlin and London. With the
Kaiser's telegram, though mild in tone and congratulatory
in substance, the fat was in the fire, patriotic Germans
cheering themselves hoarse that mighty Britain had been
defied and patriotic Englishmen also losing the voice of
reason by screaming that Queen Victoria's grandson was
giving her support to England's enemies. Rival Imperial-
isms always excited and envenomed relations between
European countries, and this Anglo-German shouting
match went on with hardly a pause until the Boer War
proper broke out at the turn of the century. England
became the best-hated country in Germany, while in
England, in the first few years of the new century,
Germany took second place only to France as an un-
mannerly intruder in Britain's colonial Empire.

Yet once the Boer War and England's initial setbacks
were under way, the Kaiser showed an Anglophil attitude
of astonishing boldness. He refused to receive Kruger
on his aid-raising visits to European capitals, but decorated the British C-in-C in South Africa, Lord Roberts,
with the Order of the Black Eagle, much to the howling
disgust of his loyal subjects. Queen Victoria was deeply
touched and Uncle Edward sent a telegram expressing
gratitude to Wilhelm. When Queen Victoria lay dying in
the last days of January 1901, the Kaiser, risking further
unpopularity at home, rushed to her bedside and held her
in his arms as she breathed her last: 'She was so little—
and so light,' he said later of this moving scene he was
never able to forget. He remained in England for over

*Right: Diplomacy by dynastic meeting—the Kaiser and the Tsar
on the battleship* Moltke *during the meeting at Björkö Sound.*
Top right: *The imperial signatures on the treaty of Björkö.*
Bottom right: *A Simplicissimus comment on the Eulenburg
affair, 'It was here that the prince first declared his love for me'*

a fortnight, and public feeling in his mother's country swung round in his favour almost overnight.

'I am the balance of power,' Wilhelm told Lord Lansdowne during this stay in England, 'since the German constitution leaves foreign policy to me.' From the same period dates another, even more ominous saying of his. A German critic reproached him for not exploiting England's difficulties in South Africa to which he replied that if you wanted to challenge a great naval power, you had to have a strong fleet yourself. 'I am in no position to go beyond the strictest neutrality [he went on]. In twenty years' time when the fleet is ready, I can use another language.' The naval race between England and Germany, assuming its most acute phase with the introduction of Dreadnoughts in 1906, was doubtless the heaviest burden placed on Anglo-German and international relations the world over. Tirpitz, the able and unscrupulous architect of the new German fleet, exploited the fact that with the appearance of the Dreadnoughts on the High Seas more English warships had become obsolete than German ones. The naval race, therefore, consisted in Tirpitz straining every nerve and exploiting the gullibility of German politicians and parliamentarians to get enough up-to-date Dreadnoughts built for the Fatherland as a serious challenge to Britain's dominance of the sea routes of the world. That dominance was for the British Isles a matter of life and death, so that the German challenge became increasingly regarded as a direct threat to British freedom of economic and commercial self-determination. 'The Royal Navy,' said Winston Churchill in 1912, 'is a dire necessity, the German fleet a luxury.'

So there is a direct line from the shock of the Kruger telegram to the excitement over the Tangiers visit, with the result that British suspicions of Germany were raised to government level where they remained. After Tangiers Admiral Fisher wrote to Lansdowne (who even at this time was turning down to Delcassé's requests for a full alliance) that: 'All I hope is that you will send a telegram to Paris that the English and French fleets are *one*. We should have the German fleet, the Kiel Canal, and Schleswig-Holstein in a fortnight.' Notions of this sort were plentifully aired in the popular press and so provided German chauvinists, Navy League warriors, and Pan-Germans with rich ammunition.

Furthermore, men who regarded Germany as the greatest menace of the future, increasingly moved into important posts at the Admiralty and the Foreign Office.

Right: *Patriotic fervour in 1913 — at the unveiling of the monument commemorating the victory over Napoleon I at Leipzig*

In 1905 Sir Thomas Sanderson left the Foreign Office. He was among the last representatives of an older, less emotional, more objective school of diplomacy. In one of his last policy papers, Sir Thomas wrote that Germany as a new power was naturally impatient to fulfil her aspirations, especially as she suffered from the insecurity of her position between the two allied Great Powers of France and Russia. He hoped that gradually her demand for colonies would become less noisy and assertive while he also hoped that Britain would desist from the susceptibilities and jealousies she had shown in the past.

In these years between Tangiers and the outbreak of war the Kaiser, and with him his Reich, had been through a number of unnerving crises at home. In 1907 Maximilian Harden provoked legal proceedings against Philipp Eulenburg, now a prince and still the Kaiser's close companion, by slandering him in the pages of *Die Zukunft*. We need not be concerned with the unedifying details of this *cause célèbre* that dragged on for too long and involved a number of Eulenburg's and the Kaiser's friends. Harden maintained throughout that he had acted as he did not because of Eulenburg's homosexual tendencies, but because, as the leader of an idolatrous and sentimentalising court clique he and they interposed themselves between the Kaiser and the nation and harmed the normal governmental machinery. Harden and Holstein behind him used the unfortunate Eulenburg as a stick with which to beat the Kaiser and his Court. The Kaiser did not hesitate to disown and drop the man who had been close to him for twenty years. Eulenburg evaded the penalties of the law by falling gravely ill and disappeared from public life, his wife standing by him to the last. Medical men apart, whose testimony we do not possess at present, Philipp Eulenburg was perhaps the only man in Germany who had intimate knowledge of the Kaiser's temperamental failings and nervous disorders and knew that in moments when the making of decisions could not be avoided, the Kaiser tended to suffer brainstorms and collapse into helplessness.

The worst error of all

The worst crisis of the reign occurred in the following year when on 28th October 1908 *The Daily Telegraph* carried an interview the Kaiser had given to an Englishman who had been his host at Highcliffe Castle. In it, the Kaiser, reviewing Anglo-Kaiser relations from the Boer War to his latest speech at the Guildhall, described himself as a true friend of England who time and again had given his motherland the benefit of his advice and support. Although this had gone against public feeling in Germany, he was still prepared to do so, even

though his patience with being constantly and deliberately misunderstood was wearing a little thin.

The most devastating aspect of this interview was that within his own terms of reference the Kaiser was absolutely sincere, and seriously expected to score a memorable international success from the publication of these remarks. In the event, he caused a political uproar at home by his references to his pro-British feelings and actions, while the effect on British opinion with its mixture of self-praise and vague offers of co-operation were received, to say the least, with the opposite of gratitude. When on 10th/11th November 1908 the interview was debated in the Reichstag, the Conservatives, true to their proven form, outdid the Social Democrats in the violence of their attack on the Kaiser, describing him as 'alienated from his people', and separated from them 'by a thick English fog'. Chancellor von Bülow, to whom the Kaiser again quite properly had sent the interview for his approval before publication, had at the time raised no objections, but later produced the excuse that he had not read it, being on leave at the time. In the Reichstag debates, he came down on the side of the critics, though naturally in more temperate language, but otherwise throwing his All-Highest Master to the Conservative and other wolves. With hypocritical effrontery, this dishonest and conceited trimmer promised the Reichstag to present the Kaiser with a sort of ultimatum either to show greater constitutional responsibility or face the fact that 'neither I nor my successors can shoulder our duties'. The Kaiser gave the promise. After a period of nervous prostration and thoughts of abdication, he resiliently recovered and sacked Bülow who, in passing the buck for the publication of the interview, had certainly been guilty of a grave dereliction of duty. The damage done to the Kaiser's position and prestige by Bülow's frivolous mishandling of the whole affair was permanent. Max Weber, the father of modern sociology and determined critic of the Second Reich, said that Germany was rightly held in contempt the world over because 'we put up with the regime of a man like him . . . we are being ostracised because that man rules over us in the way he does and we accept, even excuse it . . .' And another critic said: 'We are the best administered and worst governed country in the world.'

Bülow was succeeded by Chancellor Theobald von Bethmann Hollweg and world war. Still during the Bülow era, the Franco-Russian alliance had been considerably strengthened and England, only twenty years earlier the

Left: The Father of his people. The Kaiser talks to a dockyard worker. Wilhelm could show very great personal charm

Englisches Flotten-Bau-Programm.

Deutsches

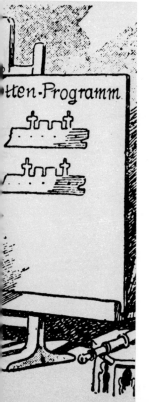

traditional enemy of both, had drawn closer to it, though not without several galling reservations. Yet, in all things except Anglo-German naval rivalry, international relations improved in the last four years before 1914. Germany and France in 1911 at last settled the Moroccan dispute, although Germany had reopened the second round with yet another *coup de théatre* by dispatching a gunboat, the *Panther,* to Agadir, a Moroccan port on the Atlantic coast. The French Premier in 1911 was Joseph Caillaux, by birth a member of the upper bourgeoisie of wealth, but by conviction a Radical who shocked France to the core with his plan to introduce income tax. Using unconventional methods and largely going behind the back of his foreign minister and the Quai d'Orsay, he established a working partnership with the new German foreign minister, Kiderlen-Wächter. In Berlin, Caillaux had the invaluable assistance of one of the period's most able and experienced diplomats, Jules Cambon. An agreement was at last signed in November 1911 by which for the acquisition of certain parts of the Congo Germany renounced all further claims in Morocco. The new agreement was signed on 4th November 1911, and the Kaiser warmly congratulated Kiderlen upon 'the termination of this delicate affair'. The negotiations had been long-drawn out, often coming close to the danger zone uppermost in the European mind, but successful in the end. Jules Cambon, on the day of signing sent Kiderlen his photographic portrait inscribed with *à mon terrible ami* and Kiderlen returned the compliment with a pleasant *à mon aimable ennemi* on his photograph.

The Franco-German accord on Morocco and the Congo, did not for long reduce the political tensions and antagonism between the two countries. *Panther* pouncing on Agadir, like the Kaiser's visit to Tangiers, had had a shock-effect in France and England that could not be wiped out by diplomatic compromise alone. In France, the last three years before 1914 witnessed an astonishing upsurge of a national revival, especially among the young pupils at the colleges and universities. Caillaux fell from the Premiership, although he returned as minister of finance, but his policy of peaceful collaboration with France's mighty neighbour across the Rhine was at an end. In 1913 Poincaré, a native of despoiled Lorraine, replaced the mild and conciliatory Fallières as President of the Republic. In his first year at the Elysée, the French Chamber discussed the famous bill of *les trois ans,*

Top: *The Kaiser talks to Admiral Tirptiz, father of the Imperial navy (right) and launches another battleship (left).* **Bottom:** *A German comment on the naval race: Edward says: 'Your little marine masterpiece is too ambitious, keep it as a study'*

105

putting up conscription from two to three years. There were cries of indignation from army barracks verging on the mutinous, but there were also expressions of a new mentality and emotionalism among the young, for which the following petition to the government from the *lycée* Condorcet may be taken as typical:

'We, the undersigned, the soldiers of tomorrow, wish to assure you that, for the life and glory of France, they are joyfully ready to sacrifice three years of their youth.'

Not that the law of three years' service did not lead to a major parliamentary battle. Jean Jaurès, the most sincere and courageous Socialist of his generation, spoke with tremendous passion in favour of a nation in arms as opposed to creating a professional army, *une armée de métier,* by keeping young proletarians under the colours for three years. The old-established reluctance of the French General Staff to arm the proletariat, which had been one of the major causes of the defeat in 1870, came under renewed attack, but the new mood in France, made impatient by youth 'embracing', as Abel Bonnard put it in 1912, 'the savage poetry of war', pushed Socialism out of the way, and the three year law was passed on 7th August 1913.

Tangiers and Agadir, as we have seen, made the Anglo-French *entente* a major factor in the continental situation created by German military might and aspirations to global hegemony. Tsarist Russia, meanwhile, had also achieved a closer understanding with Britain, although both partners, the Liberal Government in general and Sir Edward Grey in particular, continued to refuse an open and unambiguous alliance.

A surface improvement

Relations between England and Germany improved on the surface after Edward VII's death in 1910. King George V and the Kaiser stood together in Westminster Hall before the coffin of the new king's father, the Kaiser's uncle, and in a public gesture the Kaiser proffered George V his right hand which the latter warmly shook. A year later the Kaiser came again to London to attend the unveiling of the Queen Victoria Memorial in front of Buckingham Palace. In 1913, King George and Queen Mary went to Berlin to be present at the wedding of the Kaiser's only daughter to Ernest, Duke of Cumberland and heir to the vanished kingdom of Hanover. These momentary gestures greatly satisfied the dynast in the Kaiser at a time when his fellow-dynast, Tsar Nicholas (another guest at the wedding), had bound himself so irrevocably to the revitalised Republic of France. As for the presence

Right: *Dynastic celebration in 1913—the Tsar drives through Berlin on his arrival at the wedding of the Kaiser's daughter*

of the British monarch in the German capital, Sir Edward Grey had gone to some length to turn it into a private family occasion rather than a state visit.

The year 1913 saw also the twenty-fifth jubilee of the Kaiser's accession, it was the centenary year of the wars of liberation from Napoleon I and so provided occasions for countless patriotic celebrations, parades, unveiling of monuments, and the like. Bethmann Hollweg had by now been Chancellor for four years, but although he had in one or two brave speeches in the Reichstag pilloried the Conservative opposition, it had become clear that, efficient administrator though he was, he was as incapable as his predecessors of achieving the adjustment between particularist Prussia and the Reich that would have toppled the former from its unnatural hegemony.

Since 1905, Chief of the German General Staff was the younger von Moltke, nephew of the victor of 1866 and 1870 from whom, however, he had inherited little else but the Moltke estate at Kreisau in Silesia. He had succeeded Schlieffen. The latter's famous plan of defeating the French by a vast outflanking and encircling movement across Belgium and Northern France, was by 1914 still the General Staff's most sacred dogma. In Schlieffen's and his successor's mind, swift defeat of the French in the West was to be followed by a war of annihilation against the Russians in the East. The psychological and political insanity of preparing for a war on two fronts was at the base of all German military planning since Schlieffen had developed his strategic notions from the late 1890s onwards. The old Prussian tradition of permitting the army to work in a closely-guarded vacuum without interference from politicians and parliamentarians had grown out of all proportion under the Kaiser's reign. He similarly forbade all ministerial or diplomatic intervention in his naval programme.

Having in the period of the Balkan and Italian-Turkish Wars given his support to settle these problems by diplomacy and conference, the Kaiser in 1913 abruptly changed his tune. Having said in 1912 that the Russo-Austrian rivalry in the Balkans did not involve vital German interests, he told the Austrian war-monger No 1, General Conrad von Hötzendorf, that should Austria plan aggression against Serbia and the greater Serbia movement under Russian protection and encouragement, they could count on Germany's full support. 'I shall regard any suggestion that may reach me from the Austrian Foreign Ministry as a command.' Jules Cambon, who had known the Kaiser better than any other foreign diplomat, wrote to the Quai d'Orsay:

'The Kaiser has ceased to be a friend of peace. His personal influence has been exerted on many crucial

occasions, but he has come to think that war with France is inevitable. As he advances in years, the reactionary tendencies of the Court, and especially the impatience of the soldiers, obtain a greater hold over his mind. Perhaps he feels some slight jealousy of the popularity of his son who flatters the passions of the Pan-Germans.'

Like Cambon, King Albert of the Belgians had hitherto regarded Wilhelm II as a man of peace. After a visit to Potsdam late in 1913, the King told friends that he found the Kaiser 'over-excited, entirely won over to the plans of the Generals, and regards war as necessary and inevitable'. In the *Echo de Paris*, the veteran Catholic Conservative Albert de Mun wrote: 'All Europe, uncertain and troubled, makes ready for war, which it regards as inevitable, without knowing its immediate cause . . .'

The deluge begins

The immediate cause was provided by the assassination at Sarajevo in Austrian Bosnia of the heir to the throne of the Habsburgs, the Archduke Franz Ferdinand, and his morganatic consort. A Bosnian teenager, fanaticised by the mystique of a Serbian secret society, succeeded with a few shots in setting Europe on the road to destruction and ruin from which it has never recovered. The series of chain reactions that culminated in the various ultimata and declarations of war early in August began with an incident that, to the present writer at least, is both typical and inexplicable. On 5th July the Kaiser received at Potsdam the Austrian ambassador who brought with him an autograph letter from Franz Joseph and a memorandum from the Austrian government. Both documents stated that relations with Serbia had now reached breaking point. The Kaiser read them in a grave and serious mood. He pointed out that a punitive invasion of the kingdom of Serbia whose collective guilt the Austrian documents alleged, could lead to international complications. Before giving his answer, the Kaiser went on, it was his duty to consult Chancellor Bethmann, who had been summoned for later that afternoon. The ambassador stayed to luncheon. *After the meal,* the Kaiser, abandoning constitutional propriety, completely changed his tune. He authorised the ambassador to assure his Emperor that, despite menacing complications, he could count on Germany's unconditional support. As for consulting Bethmann, it could be taken for granted that he would give his consent to all he, his Kaiser, had said. For the rest, it was imperative that Austria acted promptly.

Left: Loyal celebration in 1913—a Berlin street decorated for the twenty-fifth anniversary of the Kaiser's accession

What had caused this dramatic change of front? Was it due to the Kaiser's temperamental instability and emotionalism? Or had he, between audience and luncheon, hastily consulted someone – the Kaiserin? General von Plessen or any other member of his military household who happened to be on duty at the *Neues Palais* that day? From none of these, particularly not from the Kaiserin who always roundly condemned anything that smacked of diminishing dynastic omnipotence, would he have received encouragement for calling the Chancellor in. At any rate, in that moment of time, when he changed once more from constitutional to dynastic sovereign he brought war, so far as Germany and Austria-Hungary were concerned, immeasurably nearer than he realised. The generals could have their war as long as they had a 'strong' monarch above them instead of one who interposed between them and their plans, his constitutional advisers, as the Kaiser had intended to do before luncheon on 5th July.

Bethmann Hollweg appeared at the *Neues Palais* later in the afternoon and confirmed in every detail the blank cheque for independent action the Kaiser had given to the ambassador and his government. The Chancellor expressed his full support to the Austrian ambassador again the following day. From then onwards, political activity in Berlin and Vienna could be called a conspiracy between the military and politicians to prevent Kaiser and Chancellor from withdrawing from the advanced position they had both taken up *vis-à-vis* the Austrian government. The conspiracy certainly succeeded with Bethmann Hollweg who favoured a local war that would restore Austria's waning prestige and power and opposed, as humiliating for Austria, the calling of a diplomatic conference. To his close associate Kurt Riezler, he is reported as saying on 20th July that he saw 'a doom greater than human power hanging over Europe and our own people'. In this fatalistic frame of mind, he gave but the mildest token-support to all efforts at mediation that reached him, particularly from Grey in London. When finally the possibility arose that England might come in on the Franco-Russian side if the conflict with Serbia broadened into a major European war involving France, his warnings to Vienna became more urgent and insistent, but it was too late.

Left: *The common touch. The Kaiser and his sons receive New Year greetings from the people outside Berlin castle*

Chapter 7
Downfall and Retirement

The Kaiser's efforts to evade the European complications he had foreseen, were, not those of a politician, but of a dynast. He thought that a word in season from him to Tsar Nicholas, King George V, the Austrian Emperor, and the kings of Italy, Rumania, and Bulgaria would prevent the conflagration. When his ambassador's dispatches from London made it clear that England was not prepared to abandon her friendship with France, his disordered mind expressed itself in what was probably one of the most hysterical marginal notes of his career. England, he scribbled furiously, was now going to proceed to strangle German political and economic life: 'A magnificent achievement; [he went on] which even those for whom it means disaster are bound to admire. Even after his death Edward VII is stronger than I who am still alive. . . .' And he ended up by saying that German consuls and agents must get going a vast conflagration throughout the whole Mohammedan world 'against this hated, unscrupulous, dishonest nation of shopkeepers – since if we are going to bleed to death, England must at least lose India'.

Nothing could make the fundamental impossibility of the Second Reich clearer than the hapless, fatalistic, and defeatist attitudes taken by Kaiser and Chancellor in the face of the great test of war. The total failure of the Reich's political leadership to tame the magniloquent figure at the top into a constitutional ruler within the law, had made it possible for the specialists of the German General Staff to enforce their will on an obedient nation. When on 1st August 1914 the Kaiser was able to exclaim that henceforth he no longer knew parties, he only knew Germans, he gave voice to a political ideal that had fired him, his soldiers, and the nation throughout the reign. A German newspaper wrote on the same day that 'these words by the Kaiser were followed by jubilant cheering such as had never been heard before in Berlin. The enthusiastic crowds intoned patriotic songs.'

Left: Manoeuvres with live ammunition: the Kaiser and staff hard at work during one of his visits to the front early in the war

ARE YOU IN LEAGUE
WITH THE KAISER?

FOOD WASTERS,
LUXURY USERS,
AND BUYERS OF
USELESS ARTICLES.

(EXTRAVAGANT ONES)
"YES! War or no War,
We live as Usual."

(THE KAISER)
"Thank you, my Friends,
for you are indeed
my Friends."

NATIONAL SERVICE

We are able to say today that with these words the Kaiser pronounced his own abdication. In our own day, putting country above parties, has often been the prelude to despotism, Fascism, and dictatorship. It was not different in 1914. The soldiers at last were able to declare Germany to be in a state of siege, and the generals commanding the country's various military districts, known collectively as the Deputy General Staff, became absolute rulers and censors in all matters political and civil. Still called Supreme War Lord, the Kaiser had no influence whatever on the formulation of strategy or military decision-making, but became to all intents and purposes a guest, and often an inconvenient passenger, at HQs in East and West. When in the battle of Verdun Falkenhayn introduced poison gas, the Kaiser read of it afterwards in a newspaper. On angrily enquiring why he had not been consulted, it was conveyed to him that there had been no time. 'If they need me so little,' he remarked, 'I might as well live in Germany.' A fate worse than death?

The War Years

His people in four war years saw very little of their sovereign, and his entourage had the greatest difficulty in persuading him to spend more time in Berlin for the sake of showing his solidarity with his sorely suffering and increasingly deprived people. His favourite retreats were his castles at Homburg and Wilhelmshöhe where he isolated himself, but kept up a household and a retinue, including grooms and horses, that were scarcely appropriate in a famished country. His psychosomatic illnesses multiplied, lumbago, rheumatism, inflammations of the throat, trouble with his good ear all expressing his impotent loathing of war, his revulsion from seeing the effective government of the country in the hands of the military, especially of the Ludendorff-Hindenburg team, both of whom he detested. With these unnatural conditions went moods changing from despondency and gloom to equally momentary euphoria and delusions of undiminished grandeur; with it also went regular outbursts of bad temper and rudeness. While Bethmann Hollweg remained in office, the Kaiser behaved more sensibly and with greater restraint than he did when that mild and kindly tutor figure was dismissed in July 1917.

Bottom left: The Kaiser was a convenient focus for Allied propaganda as in this British poster. Top left: 'The Great Goth'; an Allied suggestion for a window in a cathedral to be built to replace those destroyed by the Germans in Belgium. Left: The warlord in action. Wilhelm inspects a regiment during one of his occasional appearances on the Western Front

His constitutional prerogative of appointing Chancellors and other servants of the state seemingly remained intact. Throughout 1915-16 he had supported Bethmann in the latter's fight against declaring unrestricted submarine warfare, which was demanded by Falkenhayn, Tirpitz, and the vocal, i.e. Pan-German, section of public opinion. Tirpitz was curtly dismissed in 1916, but on 9th January 1917 at a Crown Council held at Schloss Pless in distant Silesia, the Kaiser expressed his support for this type of warfare which all military and naval specialists had declared would lead to England's 'being forced to her knees' within four to six months. With a feeble 'If success beckons, we must do it,' Bethmann acquiesced.

Despite his defeat, he did not resign. By resigning over the U-boat issue in 1916 Bethmann could have rendered his Kaiser and country a last service of signal significance. His successors were the widely-unknown civil servant, Michaelis, whose term lasted barely three months, and then Count Hertling, a senile and servile Bavarian courtier, politician, and professor of philosophy who remained in office for eleven months.

A year later, Prince Max of Baden was appointed Chancellor. He would have been the ideal choice a year earlier, but by October 1918 the German army in the West had been decisively beaten, more so than the Allies realised. Ludendorff, who had suffered a major nervous collapse in August, by the end of September insisted that the German government instantly ask for an armistice in the West. Hertling resigned, Prince Max came in and fought Ludendorff's defeatism tooth and nail. The new Chancellor was ready to enter peace parleys forthwith, but not on the basis of admitted defeat, a policy which we now know to have had its justification since leading opinion in the West, including President Wilson's United States, expected the war to last until well into 1919 at least. Yet Ludendorff remained adamant, and Prince Max had no choice but to send the request for a suspension of hostilities to Washington. From the first, therefore, Ludendorff had stabbed Germany's civilian front in the back, depriving it of its principal bargaining counter.

The six weeks of Prince Max's government were feverishly divided into an exchange of notes between the German and American governments on the one hand, and streamlined internal reforms on the other. The transformation of the antiquated Prussian structure of the Reich, of which sensible and enlightened Germans had dreamed throughout the reign, took place in an atmosphere of threatened revolution, mutiny, and dissolving

Left: The Kaiser and the younger Moltke, his first wartime chief-of-staff, on their way to a conference early in the war

authority. Members of the Social Democratic Party as well as representatives of the left-wing liberals, had joined the government, but the Social Democrats, afraid of their own extremists, the Independents and the Spartacists, were not the asset to the new government Prince Max had hoped. Above all, there was the revelation of Germany's total military bankruptcy which after four years of censorship and fraudulent HQ communiqués, was perhaps the biggest shock of all.

The Kaiser runs away

The Kaiser, who was in Berlin throughout October, took a decision at the end of the month that was typical of the man and disastrous for the Reich—he ran away. This time he chose Hindenburg's HQ at Spa as a refuge from decision-making with the result that Prince Max's major policy objective, viz. to preserve the monarchy, already transformed out of all recognition, by inducing Kaiser and Crown Prince to abdicate in favour of a Regency, had to be negotiated by telephone. At Spa, the All Highest was surrounded by generals, including Gröner, the successor of Ludendorff sacked by Prince Max on 25th October, who at first were rigidly opposed to abdication. As news from Berlin grew more and more desperate, the Kaiser at length declared himself ready to abdicate as German Emperor, but remain King of Prussia to lead the troops back into the Fatherland. But now the generals, being more closely aware of the mood and morale of the troops than the Kaiser, felt compelled to tell Wilhelm II through the mouth of Gröner that the troops would no longer follow him and that their oath of allegiance had lost its meaning.

In the early hours of 10th November the Kaiser for the last time boarded his special train. It took him to the Dutch border where he had to spend six dreary hours waiting. Eventually permission to cross over arrived and the ex-Kaiser was escorted to Count Bentinck's chateau of Amerongen. He briskly entered his latest haven of refuge and said to his host: 'Now give me a cup of good English tea.'

Eventually, he settled at Doorn where he died on June 4th 1941. Little of interest can be said of this period of exile. He remained as self-contradictory and split against himself as ever, personally amiable and politically shallow. He did not show any traces of rethinking the ups and downs of his reign or of looking for any fault in the system, let alone in himself. Against this, it must be mentioned that when Hitler took over in Germany, the Kaiser behaved well to a number of victims of Nazi persecution. Possibly under the same heading might be mentioned a learned lecture he, as ever an ardent student

of archaeology, gave at Doorn late in 1933 before a specially invited audience of scholars and friends. His subject included a study of the origins of the swastika in prehistoric times, and in the course of it he described the version with its upper beam to the right and pointing to the West, as symbolising 'sun, summer, fame, fortune, and wealth'. The other version, at the time of the lecture figuring on every Nazi flag in Germany, with its eastwards-pointing upper beam signified 'night, misfortune, and death' in the lore of ancient lands from India and Persia to Mexico. The non-Nazi stance of the ex-Kaiser seemed assured but then, on 14th June 1940, he sent Hitler a telegram of congratulation on the German armies entering Paris.

Unlike his grandfather, the Prince Consort, the Kaiser was not a typical German; he was one of nature's cosmopolitans. He was happiest in English country-houses, and despite his congenital suspicions not only of his uncle Edward VII, but of politicians like Lord Salisbury, Winston Churchill, and Sir Edward Grey, always went out of his way to exercise his powerful charm and unaffected kindness on individual Englishmen and women. Towards visiting French generals and, when in England, towards the Empress Eugénie at Farnborough he showed exceptional courtesy, as he did to American politicians, diplomats, and visiting businessmen and technocrats. So far as the Kaiserin and his pompous court-officials would let him, he tempered the stiffness of his Court with frequent touches of a more congenial informality. He reserved his appalling rudeness and unconcealed bad temper for his own countrymen and never felt entirely at ease among the pillars and top people of the Second Reich.

At the same time he was the ideal interpreter of the Second Reich. His sense of the dramatic, riding in splendid uniform through the streets of Berlin at the head of his Guards, his well-known aversion from party politics, his brash assertions of German world policy and his much-expressed faith in the superiority of German character, efficiency, youthful aspirations, and industriousness, all reflected and mirrored what the Germans of his times liked to feel themselves to be. So novel and breath-taking were the outward trappings of the reign, so heartening his repeated insistence on Germany's outward urges and armed might, that contemporary observers became too dazzled to realise that only the style, not the substance, of the reign was new. The Kaiser was no innovator, no creative ruler like Louis XIV or

Left: *Last minute instructions. Stage manager Hindenburg humbly whispers orders to his attentive supreme warlord*

Frederick the Great, who reshaped their kingdoms governmentally and socially in accordance with the political facts of their times. Wilhelm II merely exaggerated and over-dramatised what he had inherited, his main motive being to lead the Reich in a direction that would be the precise opposite to everything his parents with their liberal English orientation had wanted. So he evolved with great aplomb his role as a personalising egocrat whose word and will was supreme law. It was the resurrection of a fake-Kaiser leading the Reich under God and Bismarck that had corrupted him as a human being—the artifice of sham absolute power that, in his case, turned him into an accomplished and very produceable actor. Throughout his reign, he received the thunderous applause of his subjects, while abroad his posturing and oratorical aggressions came to be regarded as political facts of consequence and moment. Critical contemporaries called the whole spectacular and disruptive business his 'personal rule', but the exact applicability of the term may be doubted. The strings in everything that mattered were usually pulled by other people. In the Bülow era particularly, his worst qualities were deliberately pushed into the foreground by that superficial and unscrupulous manipulator of power politics who drove the Kaiser into courses which Wilhelm's instincts told him were false and wrong. The whole ill-conceived artifice resulted, to the point of caricature, in a distortion of the function of politics in a modern and thriving state.

Off-stage, the story was different. Beneath the gorgeous and theatrical apparition of the last German Kaiser, a more human, simple, and sensible figure becomes sometimes visible, a more friendly spectre all but stifled under the Imperial purple. It would be quite feasible to assemble an anthology of some of his words and deeds in which for every five examples of outrageous inanities, one good remark, one expression indicating an excellent sense of humour (sometimes with himself as target), and one action of inconspicuous kindness and tolerance could be quoted. It is absurd to call a man like him criminal or guilty. His own and the Second Reich's share in the causes behind the outbreak of the First World War must be viewed historically, i.e. in proportion to conditions, emotions, motives, and structures in other European countries which were, during his reign, also stricken with 'the canker of a long peace'. That investigation has only just begun, and we may all expect considerable surprises.

*Top right: Will he be allowed in? The Kaiser waits at the Dutch border during his flight into exile. **Bottom right:** The Kaiser surrounded by his relatives at his last home at Doorn in Holland*

Chronology of Events

1849 After the Revolution of 1848-49 in Germany the Prussian Union Scheme is devised, providing for a large confederation, an inner one comprising non-Habsburg Germany under the leadership of Prussia and the Habsburg Monarchy remaining intact.

1850 **29th November:** the Humiliation of Olmütz: the Prussians abandon the Prussian Union and recognise the re-established Germanic Diet at Frankfurt

1850 -53 Prussia is able to thwart Austria's effort to join the Zollverein. In 1853 Hanover, Brunswick, and Oldenburg join it

1862 **September:** Otto von Bismarck comes to power to continue the struggle against the Prussian Landtag

1863 The struggle over Schleswig and Holstein comes to a head when King Frederick VII of Denmark announces the annexation of the duchy of Schleswig to Denmark

1864 In renewed war the Danes are defeated and the duchies of Schleswig, Holstein, and Lauenburg are surrendered to Austria and Prussia by the peace of Vienna on 30th October

1866 **June-August:** the Seven Weeks' War: on 3rd July the Prussians win the victory of Königgrätz

1867 The North German Confederation comes into being through the work of Bismarck. There is to be a presidency held by the King of Prussia, represented by a chancellor, a federal council *(Bundesrat)*, and a lower house *(Reichstag)*

1870 -71 The Franco-Prussian War: on 1st September 1870 the army of Napoleon III surrenders to the Prussians at Sedan

1871 **18th January:** the second German Empire is founded and Wilhelm I is proclaimed German Emperor at Versailles
28th January: Paris capitulates to the Prussians and on 10th May a peace treaty is signed at Frankfurt

1871 -83 The *Kulturkampf:* Bismarck's struggle with the Catholic Church

1890 **18th March:** Bismarck resigns after a rift with Wilhelm II over the anti-Socialist law and Wilhelm's dissatisfaction with his policy toward Russia and desire for closer relations with Austria and Britain

1890 The chancellorship of General von Caprivi begins

1894 -1900 The chancellorship of Prince Chlodwig zu Hohenlohe-Schillingsfürst

1900 The chancellorship of Count von Bülow begins

1905 Wilhelm's visit to Tangiers precipitates the first

1905 -6 Wilhelm's visit to Tangiers precipitates the first Moroccan crisis

1907 Maximilian Harden slanders Philipp Eulenburg in *Die Zukunft* and as a result legal action is taken

1909 The chancellorship of Bethmann Hollweg begins

1910 Wilhelm attends the funeral of Edward VII in London
4th-5th November: Tsar Nicholas II and his foreign minister Sazonov visit Wilhelm at Potsdam

1911 **1st July:** the second Moroccan crisis: the German gunboat *Panther* arrives at Agadir

1913 King George and Queen Mary are guests with Tsar Nicholas at the wedding of Wilhelm's only daughter to Ernest, Duke of Cumberland

1916 **14th March:** Admiral von Tirpitz resigns in protest against Wilhelm's unwillingness to make full use of German sea-power

1918 **11th November:** an armistice ends the First World War

Top: Wilhelm as Lieutenant of the Imperial Guard Regiment (left); Princess Victoria Louise, only daughter of Wilhelm (middle); the Zollverein stand at the Great Exhibition of 1851 (right). **Centre:** *Alfred Krupp (left); inside his munitions factory (middle); German industry in the 1870s (right).*
Bottom: *the monument to commemorate the battle of Leipzig (left); the Kaiser posing for an equestrian portrait (middle); 'The Fate of Animals' by Franz Marc (right)*

Index of main people, places, and events

124

Author's suggestions for further reading

Works on Wilhelm II and his era in English are, almost without exception, 'secondary' works based not on original documentary research but on the memoirs and apologia of prominent contemporaries. The most recent study of this type is Michael Balfour's *The Kaiser and his Times* (London 1964) which says in essence that the Kaiser was not a totally bad man, even from the English point of view, while I. von Kürenberg's *The Kaiser* (English translation 1952) tells us that in many ways he was as admirable man, especially from the German point of view. Virginia Cowles' *The Kaiser* (London 1963) pleasantly rambles through the warmed-up gossip of six or seven decades. It sold well in its German translation as did Emil Ludwig's *Wilhelm Hohenzollern* (New York 1927) in its English one. The best study in German is Erich Eyck's *Das Persönliche Regiment Wilhelms II* (Zurich 1948) which is richer than the others in serious research, although it is written in the tone of voice of an angry National Liberal in 1909. One could have done with more liberal anger and action before 1914, but the attitude looks sterile in the 1960s.

The interested reader is therefore still compelled to piece together a comprehensive picture of the man and his times from a wide variety of works by scholars and historians describing this or that episode. Chancellors Hohenlohe, Bülow, Bethmann Hollweg, Hertling and Prince Max von Baden have all left their reminiscences in one form and another. Of these, only Bülow's fraudulent and absurdly conceited volumes have left any impact (English translation 1931). The diaries of Admiral von Müller, the Kaiser's Chief of Naval Cabinet, have also been translated into English as *The Kaiser and his Court* (1961) and, despite indifferent editorship and translation, are indispensable for the Kaiser in wartime. This may also be said of Prince Max's Memoirs published in English in 1928 and of deep interest for the light it throws on the Kaiser's character, including during the abdication crisis of 1918.

A vast amount of unpublished material remains to be investigated in numerous European and North American archives before we may expect a convincing portrait of the mind and conduct of a man whom it is easy to underrate and easier still to condemn.

Harold Kurtz studied history at Geneva University, and came to live in England in 1936. He worked for the BBC during the war and at the Nuremberg Trials from 1946 to 1949. He has written a number of articles for *History Today*, reviewed books in several journals, and written scripts for the BBC. His books include: *The Trial of Marshal Ney* and *The Empress Eugénie.*

JM Roberts, General Editor of the *Macdonald Library of the 20th Century*, is Fellow and Tutor in Modern History at Merton College, Oxford. He is also General Editor of Purnell's *History of the 20th Century* and Joint-Editor of the *English Historical Review*, and author of *Europe 1880-1945* in the Longman's History of Europe. He has been English Editor of the *Larousse Encyclopedia of Modern History*, has reviewed for *The Observer, New Statesman,* and *Spectator,* and given talks on the BBC.

Library of the 20th Century

Publisher: John Selwyn Gummer
Editor: Christopher Falkus
Executive Editor: Jonathan Martin
Editorial Assistant: Jenny Ashby
Designed by: Brian Mayers/ Germano Facetti
Design: Henning Boehlke
Research: Sue Graham

Pictures selected from the following sources:

Archiv Kurt Desch 35
Archiv Gerstenberg 57 75 93 123
Author's Collection 99 118
Bayer. Armeemuseum, Ingolstadt 26
Bundesarchiv, Koblenz 25 45 66 88 89 93 104 128
Diagram 30 50 82
Goettinger Verlagsanstalt 90
Historisches Bildarchiv L. Handke 35
Illustrated London News 14 22 32 123
Imperial War Museum 114
Jugend 76
Kunsthalle, Hamburg 18
Le Petit Journal 62
Le Rire 87
L'Illustration 122
Thomas Mann Archiv, Zürich 81
Mansell Collection 123
Museum für Hamburgische Geschichte 75
National Galerie, Berlin 21
Paul Popper 8 60 64 70 122
Radio Times Hulton Picture Library 36 40 42 46 49 54 67 69 104 110 112 123
Roger-Viollet 116
Simplicissimus 84 89
Staatsbibliothek Berlin Bildarchiv 16 28 38 57 58 67 73 101 121
Städt. Galerie im Lenbachhaus, Munich 52
Südd-Verlag, Munich 10 12 41 67 73 79 80 87 99 121
Hans Tasiemka 35 64 75 93 94 99
Ullstein 1 4 7 10 16 41 68 80 89 94 96 107 108
Verlag Weineck 17 81 122 123